D1517831

Ethel K. Smith Library

Wingate University
Wingate, North Carolina 28174

I'LL LOVE YOU FOREVER, ANYWAY

I'LL LOVE YOU FOREVER, ANYWAY

Edith Kunhardt Davis

DONALD I. FINE, INC.

New York

WINGATE UNIVERSITY LIBRARY

Copyright © 1995 by Edith Kunhardt Davis

All rights reserved, including the right of reproduction in whole or in part in any form. Published in the United States of America by Donald I. Fine, Inc. and in Canada by General Publishing Company Limited.

Library of Congress Catalogue Card Number: 94-061913
ISBN: 1-55611-450-8

Manufactured in the United States of America

10 9 8 7 6 5 4 3 2 1

Designed by Irving Perkins Associates

Photo credits:

Frontispiece by William J. McGuire.
p. 78 Beloit College photo.
p. 119 by Joan Paton Tilney.
p. 174 by William J. McGuire.
p. 177 photographer unknown.
All other photographs were taken by the author.

to
H.P.

ACKNOWLEDGMENTS

I want to thank Jane Dystel, my agent, and Don Fine, my publisher, for their faith in my work.

I'm grateful to God for giving me the courage to endure, to my family for their love, to my friends for their steadfast devotion, to everyone who carried me through by sharing their experience, strength, and hope.

Specifically, I'm indebted to those who read this manuscript, in whole or in part, in various stages, and in some cases, repeatedly, before it was finished, and offered their thoughts and advice: Justine Auchincloss, Peggy Casey, Bob Cranny, Kennedy Fraser, Beverly M. Galban, Mary Hedges, Kay Karlin, Racelle Larkin, Henny Mead, Joan Meisel, Gregor Roy, Betsy Smith, Ann White.

With devout thanks also for their faithful friendship: Hope Brown, Polly Cone, Eileen Farrell, Elizabeth Halsey, Susan Hirschman, Isabelle Holland, Joy Jacobs, Christine Kealy, Barbara Ludlow, Harry Ludlow, Newton McVeigh, Anne Reiniger, Frank Scott, Clare Scott, Irwin Sloan, Patty Stout, Prentice Stout, Joan Paton Tilney, Gottfried von Koschenbahr, Hank Watson.

I'm also grateful to Edie Smith for her unfailing patience and wise advice.

With special appreciation to Adrian Allen, whose extraordinary compassion has sustained me for over twenty years.

Thanks, also, to Nancy, Phil, and Ken, who have loved me all my life.

Finally, I am most grateful for the presence in my life of Martha, my tenacious, gallant, persistent, determined, indomitable, courageous, funny, lovable, loving daughter.

It is the truth that we deny which so tenderly and forgivingly picks up the fragments and puts them together again.

—Laurens Van der Post

INTRODUCTION

This book is about the year following my twenty-seven-year-old son's death. My son's name was Edward S. Davis Jr. I called him Neddy. Neddy's death was unexpected and left me in deep shock. For all my worries and fears for his life and his health, I never thought I would lose him so soon.

Six days after Neddy died, I started a journal. The outpouring that filled the pages was almost an unconscious act, like automatic writing. It was a way of saving my life, for I was swept up on a tide of bewilderment and horror, rage and fear, inconsolable sorrow and regret that threatened to cast me into oblivion. At first the writing was an attempt to set down events as they unfolded. Later I was able to pull back to a broader view which I hoped would help me make sense of Neddy's life and my own.

When I finished the journal at the end of the year following Neddy's death, it consisted of 801 typed pages. Included in it were not only an account of my grief, but the texts of all the letters Neddy had ever written me, quotes from old diaries, and excerpts from the "grief books" that I had been avidly reading. In those books I discovered that I was not alone, that most bereaved parents feel guilty, no matter what the circumstances; they often feel angry, especially at doctors. Writing helped me to study the grief process, as it were, as I endured it.

An important component of my particular story was the guilt

that I carried because I was an alcoholic parent who lived in an era when doctors did not restrict drinking during pregnancy. My fears that I might possibly have caused Neddy's heart illness—and his dyslexia—through drinking while pregnant haunted me and complicated the mourning process. It was only through the writing itself and faith in God that I was ultimately able to come to terms with this devastating burden.

After the first anniversary of Neddy's death, I began to write this book, which took two and a half years. I worked with a huge amount of material based on video and audio tapes, home movies, diaries, letters, report cards, doctors' reports, and photographs. When I started writing, I felt, as most bereaved parents do, that I was a total failure as a parent. But gradually, over time, I came to see not only my mistakes and failings, but my strengths and the depth of devotion between me and my son. It was wonderful and yet sad to reflect that we had healed so much, and then he was snatched away.

It's difficult now to remember how terrified I was to face what had happened. I needed every ounce of courage and strength I could muster to let myself review the events of Neddy's final year of life and the medical clues that had been missed. And yet forcing myself to face the truth—and, ultimately, unveiling my whole life, and Neddy's—led to peace, release, and a new point of view.

The path I took in the first year after Neddy's death, that of slowing down and immersing myself in feelings, was the path to freedom. That I took this route is momentous because I had spent much of my life trying to blot out my emotions.

I've read that T cells—the cells which supply a healthy immune system—are actually changed by writing; the immune system is actually strengthened. I believe that I gained and maintained physical health by writing the journal and this book.

I'm grateful that Neddy was my son, that I knew him. He taught me about courage and love. I don't want to forget. I'll never forget.

The initials and names that I have invented for the doctors and others are fictional and are not intended to identify any person who may have an initial or name similar to the fictional ones.

Unavoidably, in the interests of clarity, incidents and people who are very important to me have not been included in this book. Some very good friends are not mentioned at all, but they have a prominent place in my heart.

Most of all, I pray that I may help others by writing about my son's life and death.

CHAPTER ONE

Now I know why people rend their clothes, tear their hair.

Oh, Neddy. I'll never see you again.

The last time: that epic journey to the funeral home in the Bronx, stuck in traffic with the Rastafarian taxi driver at 110th Street. Finally we boarded the subway at 116th, creeping out to Parkchester. I'd last seen your motionless body in the hospital cubicle: eyes open, pupils askew, mouth ajar, stubble of beard. I sat on the footstool, unmoving, staring at you, my mouth hanging open in an identical way. Were you still warm? I couldn't touch you.

In the funeral parlor, you'd been fixed up. You looked pink, just sleeping, from far away. Closer up, you looked dead. You wore blue jeans, a pink button-down shirt, a red tie. I sat on a prie-dieu at the coffin's side and wept.

Coming out of my grim reverie and looking around the plane, I glared at cheerful families traveling together on July vacations. I was on the third leg of my journey from New York City to Cape Breton Island in Nova Scotia to visit an old friend. My twenty-seven-year-old son, Neddy, had died three weeks before.

Your anger at me brought us closer in the end. "You did this to me!" you said. "You caused my heart problem! Because of your alcoholism! You drank when you were pregnant!"

I shifted in my seat. I was wracked with guilt that my drinking might have caused the physical condition that killed Neddy.

That conversation last night with my ex-husband about our son's ashes was so surreal. How could we be discussing such a thing? How could we calmly agree that the ashes would be delivered to my ex-husband's apartment by the crematory? It was obscene.

Oddly, Neddy had talked about cremation the last time I saw him—and he wasn't even supposed to be sick. That is, the doctors hadn't diagnosed what was wrong with him. Did he somehow know he was going to die? "I want to be cremated, reduced to my carbon," he said. *Why didn't I scream and cry and grab you and tell you it wasn't O.K. to talk that way?*

The steward stopped next to my seat with the drinks cart. I chose mineral water. I hadn't had a drink of alcohol for many years. I knew I could drink alcohol if I wanted to, but I didn't choose to today, didn't even want to. I sipped the cool beverage.

C.S. Lewis said that grief feels like fear. It was true. I was suffused with low-level fear all the time. Leaning my head against the seat, I drew a deep breath and tried to relax.

Three weeks ago, on June 20, 1990, when I returned home from couples therapy with Bill, the man with whom I lived, there was a message on my answering machine. It was from Dr. G, Neddy's cardiologist. His voice said, "Your son is in intensive care at the hospital. Please call immediately."

With my heart pounding, I dialed the number. An operator answered and said she'd page the doctor for me and get him to call back. I hung up.

We waited ten minutes for his call. I scurried around, efficiently packing clothes, granola bars, and quarters for the pay phone, in case I had to stay in the hospital overnight.

The phone rang. Dr. G announced, without any preamble, using Neddy's adult nickname, "Ned is in intensive care. He had chest pains and drove in from New Jersey to meet me at the emergency ward. When he arrived his heart muscle was very weak. It was strong when I tested him two months ago. We immediately put him in intensive care."

He continued, "He had a rapid pulse and his blood pressure had dropped. He is quite sick. We suspect a bacterial infection of the aortic valve. He may have also sustained a heart attack. He is in quite serious trouble. This is not a happy state of affairs. Dr. L is his surgeon."

A surgeon? A surgeon? What for?

"We've taken cultures and they're growing," the doctor continued. "We may not know for a couple of days what the bacteria is, but we're treating him with three antibiotics." And then, ominously, "This could be fatal. He's just hanging on."

A child across the plane's aisle began to cry. The sound grated on my nerves. The cacophony of screeching child and blowing air, plus the sprightly chatter of the other passengers, sent me into sobbing. The steward knelt by my side with Kleenex and asked, "Is there anything I can do?"

"My son is dead!" I burst out, and saw the shock on his face. "No. No. Thank you," I added, absently taking the tissues and balling them in my hand as the tears slid unhindered down my cheeks.

Ashes. You're just ashes now, my son. Wearing your red tie you became ashes. Reduced to your carbon you became ashes. Why did you cancel that doctor's appointment? If you'd kept it, maybe you'd be alive.

Finally the sobs turned into gasping sighs and the tears began to dry on my face. I wiped mucus from my nose and leaned my head wearily back against the seat. I felt so alone.

Looking idly over to my left, I saw a young, bearded man at the other end of my row. There were two empty seats between us. The man reached down to pick up a box enclosed in a green chamois bag. The box seemed heavy and he set it square upon his lap. His big hands were gentle and they rested on the box tenderly. In a moment he loosened the drawstring, revealing a mottled shiny granitelike finish, then pulled the white drawstring closed again.

Glancing over at me, he noticed me staring, and murmured, "I'm takin' m' dad back home." He patted the box lovingly and smiled.

It seemed like the most incredible coincidence.

I asked to see his father's ashes and he let me hold the box. It was sealed. It had a silver plaque on it which read, ROBERT MI- CHAELS 1922–1989. I cradled it to my chest.

"What did he die of?" asked the man, whose name turned out to be Bob, when I told him about Neddy.

I struggled with the unfamiliar words, graven into my memory just three weeks ago, when it happened. "Strep viridans. It's an infection in the heart. He'd had open-heart surgery, to fix a valve, three years ago, and completely recovered. But then a bacteria got in his system. You're susceptible, when you have any kind of im- plant, to infection. He died three weeks ago."

I used to be able to say I talked to you last Monday. Now it's three Mondays ago.

"How old was he?"

"He was twenty-seven, and just settling down after finishing school late because of dyslexia. He lived in New Jersey, had a good job at a bank, and he and his girlfriend were talking about getting married."

"Oh, no." Dick sighed. He added, "It's not for us to know why, it's just for us to know that it is."

It is. It is. I know that it is.

Your puffy cheeks—stuffed with cotton? Your hands like wax, your bitten nails.

"Was he in the hospital long?" Dick asked.

"He wasn't in the hospital at all! That is, not until the day he died. He worked at his job right up until three Wednesdays ago, when he woke up with chest pains. You see, nobody had diagnosed the condition."

But I knew! I knew! I knew there was something terribly wrong! Oh, God. Why didn't I save you? Why? Why? But that doesn't matter anymore, because you're dead. The stark fact of it stopped my tor- ture cold.

"Oh, that's rough," said Dick. "At least with my dad it was expected. He was real sick with cancer."

"I'm sorry," I murmured.

I rented a car in Sydney and set out to meet my friend Dede, who lived in a Buddhist abbey on the western coast of Cape Breton Island.

I had first met Dede at the girls' boarding school we had attended in the fifties. Marooned there, for the school's strict rules did not allow us to leave often, we and our classmates had formed some of the closest friendships of our lives. Dede had found peace in her life by becoming a Buddhist nun, one of the first ordained in China in many centuries. Her Buddhist name was Pema, for short. On her path to becoming a nun she had performed 100,000 protestations, which meant throwing herself repeatedly full-length on the floor, getting up, and throwing herself down again, 100,000 times. She had also endured the burning of incense cones on her shaven head, to prove she could undergo pain and as a training to bear the suffering of the world. I had called her soon after Neddy had died and asked if I could visit for a week.

I looked at a map and chose a route to the abbey through Ingonish on the Cabot Trail. If I had known it would take me four and a half hours to get to my destination, I might have stopped at a motel, as I was still in shock. (Later, I found out that the trip usually takes two and a half hours.)

I had brought my camera, but I couldn't imagine that I would ever want to take another picture, or do anything normal ever again. However, old habits die hard, and I had been photographing since I was eleven years old. Besides, I knew I had to save my life. My life was definitely in danger—I felt as if I might die of distraction—and I instinctively knew that creative work might be a way to preserve it.

Throughout that long drive I repeatedly stopped the car, climbed out from the driver's seat, and recorded the scene. Gradually, through pondering the considerations of light and shadow, noticing the details of f-stop and focal length, hearing the shutter slide smoothly open and closed, and simply hefting the weight and smoothness of my sleek, black camera in my hand, I began to feel a certain peace.

I called the abbey from rest stops, and heard gentle Buddhist voices babbling confusing directions about the Irving gas station.

People along the way helped sort out the directions. Also, when my steering wheel locked, leaving me marooned at a rest stop, some tourists told me you have to push the brake pedal to release the wheel.

At other times, the highway was completely deserted for ten or fifteen miles at a time. I had the feeling that if I slipped off the edge of the tarmac, no one would find me until spring. And what about elks? What if I rounded a corner and smacked into an elk?

In the background, there was always Neddy. Three-year-old Neddy hugging his grandfather's Labrador retriever. Teen-aged Neddy patting a horse in Ireland. Grown-up Neddy saying, "Hey, pups," to a golden retriever on the street, and squatting down to embrace it.

Finally, I reached the other side of the island. In darkness, I turned off the main highway at the Irving station and drove on a dirt road hung on the flank of a mountain looming over the sea. At the end of the road, I came upon Pema, a dim form standing in the abbey's driveway. We embraced and she helped me carry my suitcase down the hill.

"I reached the other side . . ."

I was staying in a monk's room, which was simply furnished with a desk, a bureau, a bookcase, and a hard mattress with no box springs on a wooden platform. Pema had arranged flowers in a vase and put out a bowl of fruit. She took me down to the big kitchen on the floor below and made a meal of cheese, carrot bread, herb tea, yogurt with strawberries, raisins and nuts. I ate hungrily.

While I ate, I looked at my old friend. Pema had extremely short cropped brown hair and wore a maroon robe, which she carried draped over one arm, and a yellow high-necked sleeveless blouse. Maroon loafers peeped out from under her robes. She wore no makeup or jewelry. Her endearingly snub-nosed face was a little wrinkled, as was mine, because we were both fifty-two years old, but I would have recognized her anywhere. She was the director of the abbey, part of a Tibetan Buddhist sect. We talked a little, whispering because the rest of the occupants of the abbey were asleep, and I soon went to bed.

At 4:30 A.M. the next morning, I stood in a hall and stared out of a window. The stars were still out.

I gazed at a star.

"I want to be reduced to my carbon," you said. The only place carbon is created is in the stars. In supernovas, to be exact. That's where the stuff we're made of came from. Is that where you are now, Neddy? In the stars?

Each moment crept by.

A patch of sky over the mountain slowly, almost imperceptibly, began to turn orange. The rest of the sky was dark gray.

When Bill and I had arrived at the hospital, we took the elevator to the cardiac intensive-care unit. Waiting were my ex-husband Ned, his wife Barbara, and Neddy's girlfriend, Elizabeth.

Ned had seen Neddy just long enough to kiss him and tell him he loved him. I was glad he saw him. Neddy loved him so.

Elizabeth told me later that she also had visited Neddy in his room before I got there. He apologized to her for being sick. "I'm sorry," he said, adding, "I'll just be in overnight."

Neddy was sedated when I arrived, so I didn't see him. In a way, I didn't want to; I was scared. Later, he was on the respirator.

We began to wait.

Did I leave to make a phone call? A nurse was talking to Ned and Barbara when I returned to the waiting room, and then she started to go back inside the ICU. I followed her and told her I was Neddy's mother.

The nurse described his arrival at the hospital after driving thirty miles from New Jersey. He left his red Toyota on the street and walked into the emergency ward. He had sustained a heart attack during the trip but had enough gumption to ask, as unfamiliar doctors began to treat him, "Where are my own doctors? I want them to work on me."

"They're on their way," the nurse answered him.

Later, Neddy wanted to know, "Am I dying?"

She answered, "No."

I told her I planned to spend the night.

She declared, "You don't need to stay. He's stable right now." I remember the shock of surprise when she said it, because of what the doctor had told me on the phone. She added, "They don't use the word 'stable' lightly around here. Most of our patients are critical. He's stable."

She repeated, "Don't spend the night. He'll need you more in a couple of days, when he's feeling better. Don't exhaust yourself."

She disappeared into the ICU.

We waited.

And waited.

And waited.

The nurse appeared again. Was that when she came to me and murmured, sotto voce, "Spend the night. He's not so stable anymore"?

The tops of the birches and pines outside of the abbey had slowly become silhouetted.

The orange patch had gradually changed to streaks of pink.

Little ribbons of clouds above the streaks were illuminated on their lower borders.

Higher up, gray wisps had turned rosy.

Please. Dear God. Please help me. The pain is so great.

Now soft feathery clouds and more substantial cirruslike clouds farther away from the main light source—still hidden—picked up the delicate pink. A band of clouds low over the main source glowed brilliant on its bottom edge.

Suddenly the sky was merely beautiful, and I lost interest. I tiptoed wearily back to bed and lay there on my back until I heard two wooden sticks being gently clapped together as a wake-up call. The sound was actually, "clack, clack, boink, boink," two faint boinks after the louder initial clacks.

I joined the residents for a silent breakfast in the dining room. Someone handed me a cup and napkin and a napkin ring, and mimed that I should write my name on strips of adhesive tape. I wrote "Edith" twice and stuck the tape onto the cup and napkin ring.

After breakfast the realization struck again, and I sobbed uncontrollably in my room.

Pema said this was like dying. I should just let myself die. Because there will come a rebirth.

She would teach me how to meditate, to still my mind from the compulsive thoughts.

Exhausted by crying but unable to relax, and in a curious state of headachey limbo, I walked outside the abbey and down to the cliff's edge, near five tall flagpoles made out of not-quite-straight logs. Ocean waves broke on the rocks a hundred feet below. Farther out, the wind made shadowy moving films on water stretching to the horizon, part of the Gulf of St. Lawrence. Above, a towering piled-up cloud bank was edged with silver. To my right, in the distance, a dramatic headland loomed. Flags on the flagpoles flapped in the breeze; Canada's with its red maple leaf, the blue and white flag of Nova Scotia, the abbey's golden flag, the sun and stripes of the Shambhala flag, and a blue and yellow wave pattern flag.

I glanced back at the abbey, which had been a farm before it was acquired by the Buddhists. A large structure which had once been a barn now housed the meditation room, dormitories, and storage space. A connected structure enclosed the monastery's library, dining room, and kitchen as well as offices and more living space. All the buildings were gray with red roofs, and the windows were trimmed in red. Outside the kitchen was the garden, vegetables growing in rectangular areas divided by planks which boxed them in and prevented erosion. Higher up on the hill beyond the garden was a three-foot-high statue of the Buddha, seated in the lotus position. Smooth round stones were piled around him, and a stream trickled into a tiny pool of water. Pine trees sheltered the shrine. Above everything loomed a mountain.

After dinner Pema and I climbed down the cliff on ladders to the pebbly beach.

I told her how Dr. G had reappeared in the hospital waiting room and announced that they were going to try to insert a pump into Neddy's heart, in order to take the strain off it. The only trouble was that the heart muscle was very weak, because of virulent bacteria.

After Dr. G left the room, Bill leaned back in a chair with his feet propped up on another one, and closed his eyes.

I stared at a magazine.

Ned worked on legal papers.

Barbara went off to get coffee.

Elizabeth paced back and forth.

After a long time, Barbara came back with the coffee.

Elizabeth and I walked out in the hall. We decided to send strength to Neddy. Standing there with my eyes closed, I beamed him steadfastness, hope, love. Soon an image of a coffin being rolled down a church aisle entered my mind. The coffin was parallel to me, as if I were viewing it from a pew.

A few minutes later Dr. G entered the waiting room. "I have terrible news." Or something like that. I remember thinking how trite the sentence was. Then he said Neddy had died.

Elizabeth burst into loud sobs and ran out of the room.

Dr. G rambled on and on about how the heart gave out. "If only he'd come in sooner," he said. Seated, I clutched Bill's shirt, touching the skin of his back beneath it, and moaned periodically. Ned and Barbara listened, standing. When Dr. G finished, Ned said, "I know you did everything you could. Thank you very much," and shook his hand.

BULLSHIT! I thought.

"If only he'd come in sooner," Dr. G repeated.

You bastard! You bastard! Sooner! How could he have known to come in sooner?

Ned and I hugged, my reading glasses on a string around my neck pressed painfully between us. "I'm sorry," he said. "I'm sorry," I murmured, also.

We went to see Neddy, twisting through the corridors. He was lying on a bed in a cubicle in the intensive care unit. The sheet was pulled up to his chin. There was a bump where his hands were folded on his chest under the sheet. His mouth hung open slackly.

Ned went directly to Neddy's head, kissed him, stared briefly, turned, and left the room.

Bill and Barbara stood quietly, then also turned and exited.

Elizabeth touched Neddy's face with her hand, tweaked his nose. She said something to him. Then she came around the bed to where I stood, hugged me, and asked, "Are you all right?" I stood numbly, speechless, while she clasped me. She left the room.

I sat down on the step stool, the step stool with black corrugated rubber on its steps, and stared at him, my mouth hanging open in an identical slack way.

After a while I noticed, between the folds of a green curtain, a nurse staring at me from the next cubicle as she cared for a patient.

Finally another nurse entered the room. I was standing by the bed. "I can't leave," I murmured.

"You don't want to remember him like this, do you?" she inquired. I looked at Neddy. He was dead. His eyes were open a crack and stared vacantly in different directions. I turned and left.

Dr. G and everyone else was in the hall. He asked Ned and me if we wanted a post-mortem.

Ned didn't. I wanted one, but I didn't dare speak up. *To find out what happened. Also to help others. You always wanted to help others.*

Dr. G said, firmly, "If it were my son I wouldn't do a post-mortem. He's been through enough." I felt a flash of anger. Why did he say that? And who cared if Neddy was cut up now? He was just dead meat.

Ned suggested a popular funeral home. "I hate it," I said. "It's a body mill. I bet our church has a funeral place affiliated with it." Dr. G said he'd call them.

We all marched out of the restricted area.

When we got out to the waiting room again, Ned gestured earnestly. "Well, there'll be the five of us," he said about attendance at the funeral. He couldn't seem to think of any more people who might come. "Gaily maybe," he mused about his sister.

"Ned, I think you're in shock," I said. "I know I am. One thing

I'm sure of is that the funeral will be huge. Neddy had so many friends. And at least a hundred of my friends will be there."

Ned looked at me unbelievingly.

We tried to call our daughter Martha in California. Ned punched in his charge card code, then her number. I held the receiver and spoke in a tense tone to her answering machine. "Call me any time tonight. I'll be home by eleven-thirty." It was still only ten of eleven. Neddy had died twenty minutes before.

Bill held my hand in the taxi. We unlocked the apartment door and went in. It was 11:05. We had left at seven-thirty. Everything looked the same.

Later, Martha called me. I couldn't even attempt a preamble. "Neddy died," I said. "Please sit down," I added. I moaned into the phone, rhythmically.

Pema and I were silent for a long time. I felt strangely removed, and my head throbbed.

Then, "What's the point of it all?" I bleated out, plaintively.

"The point is the sacredness of now," Pema answered.

CHAPTER TWO

I spilled the vodka into a glass (a brownish crust of old juice lined the rim), then added V-8 juice. The first sip relieved the pressure in my head. My hands shook as I lifted the glass up for a second slug. My stomach churned, but a peace began. I lit a cigarette, and sighed.

"Mummy, when are we going to the beach?" nine-year-old Martha asked, appearing at the kitchen door.

"Later, later," I mumbled, trying to conceal the drink, as it was only ten in the morning. "Go back outside and finish that puzzle," I added.

"I have finished it. I'm hot. I want to go to the beach," Martha whined.

The screen door slammed. My seven-year-old-son, Neddy, rushed into the room. "A chipmunk ran across my foot!" Neddy squeaked in his high voice. "When are we going to the beach? It's hot," he added.

"I told you, later!" I shrilled, slamming my cigarette out in the ashtray. "It's only ten in the morning and we have to clear this place up before the owners get back. Come on, Martha, you strip the beds. Neddy, empty the wastebaskets. I'll sweep."

"Ohhhh. You promised we could go to the beach early today," Neddy complained.

"Do you want a spanking? I said empty the wastebasket!" I ordered, the pressure in my head mounting to an unbearable level. I openly took a large gulp of the drink, the vodka burning as it went down.

An hour and a half later the house looked better. The flutters in my stomach had quieted down, and now I felt a gentle floating feeling. Only a couple of drinks, on top of last night's excesses, had made me woozy. In fact, I couldn't remember last night at all after about 7:00 P.M., when I switched to bourbon from beer. But I must have gotten the children to bed all right, and myself, because I woke up in bed in my cigarette-hole-dotted nightgown, and the children woke up in their beds.

"Into the car, kids," I called, gathering up some beach towels. I carefully stowed three giant-sized cans of beer in the bag along with the suntan lotion.

"I'm bringing the tire today," said Neddy, dragging an inflated inner tube to ride on in the surf.

"Partha, can you carry the sandwiches?" I asked Martha, using her nickname. She picked up the wrapped peanut butter and jelly sandwiches and started toward the kitchen door.

On my way out, feeling a familiar shakiness, I shook a pale blue 10-milligram Valium out of a bottle into the palm of my hand. As a shortcut, I chewed it up dry, gagging a little, and locked the house after me.

As I left by the back door, I checked the thermometer outside the kitchen window. Ninety degrees. I had awakened drenched, and now sweat coated my body. This was nothing new. I sweated both winter and summer. My hands were slippery on the steering wheel of the car.

The parking lot at the beach was scorching. I was lucky to get a parking place. The sand sizzled the bottom of my feet as I made my way, with gear hanging off me, toward the water. The kids ran to its edge.

I tipped the beach chair upside down, embedding its aluminum tubing in the sand, then spread out my towel. I leaned back against the slanted webbed plastic of the inverted seat back and sighed. Now there was the business of lighting a cigarette in the wind. Ahh. A deep inhale. Peace.

"It's neat!" Neddy said, throwing himself down next to me and dripping all over my towel. "Come on in."

"I will, in a minute."

"O.K. There are some red jellyfish, but not too many," he added, and ran back to the water.

"Just what I need," I muttered. I flipped open a beer, took a long swallow. I kept an eagle eye on the children as they played in the wash from the waves. Then Neddy dug in the sand and Martha played a game with the water, rushing forward when the waves drew out, and retreating when the next wave came in.

Now for the Bain de Soleil. I rubbed the greasy orange gel on my arms, legs, and chest. It blocked my pores so that I was much hotter when I used it, but it certainly helped me to get a deep tan.

Martha threw herself down and picked up her book, began to read. She was reading Madeline L'Engle and was thoroughly hooked. "You ought to go in, Mummy," she murmured absently.

I took another long pull at the beer and smothered my cigarette in the sand. Then I pulled myself up to my feet. I really am getting too heavy. This size sixteen is almost too tight. Oh, well, I'll go on a diet next week.

It was cooler at the water's edge. I plunged into the surf. The water was deliciously cool as it hit my scalp. Neddy scrambled into the water next to me, his pipelike arms and legs churning. He swam to me and grabbed me with his arms and legs, hanging off me like a crab. We bobbed in the waves, lifting up when a big wave broke and just touching the sandy bottom in the troughs. Martha splashed out into the water and also grasped me with her arms and legs. I could feel myself submerging when a big wave surged in. I struggled to escape the arms and legs, and finally freed myself, laughing. "Later, later," I said. "That was fun."

Back on my towel, I opened another beer and sat down. This was more like it. I allowed my eyes to close halfway since the children were definitely not playing in the water.

"I want a snow cone!" Neddy's voice hit me like a cold shower and my head jerked up.

"And I want an almond crunch," Martha added.

"Can we have some money for the ice cream man?"

I saw the ice cream truck parked at the entrance to the beach. "O.K., children," I said, digging in my bag for change. "But remember, you have to eat all your lunch. And you can't have another ice cream later if you have one now. Maybe you'd better sit down and have your sandwiches, then you can get the ice cream."

"O.K.," Martha said, sitting down.

"I don't want to," said Neddy, but he sat down, too.

They ate in silence. I nibbled at the corner of a sandwich, pulled on the beer. "Put the waste paper in the red bag," I said, indicating the cooler bag.

When I finished a double fudge sundae from the ice cream truck, I was tired. The third beer was all gone, and now I needed to sleep.

"Just one more dip to get the sand off, and then it's back to the house," I said.

"Awww, it's too soon. Please let us stay," begged Neddy.

"Please," Martha pleaded.

"We'll come back later," I said, knowing we wouldn't. I submerged myself in the water again, and felt a stinging like nettles along my right thigh. "Ouch!" I cried. "A red jellyfish!"

Now it really was time to go home.

Being an alcoholic made the mourning harder, because of the self-hate, the guilt, and shame that I carried around all the time. It didn't matter that I hadn't had a drink in seventeen years . . .

Accepting and admitting that I was alcoholic was the hardest thing I had ever done. Knowing that it was a disease with a distinct progression of symptoms and recognized as such by the American Medical Association helped me make the leap of faith. What was the most shameful secret of my life became the beginning of everything, for all good things sprang from that time, seventeen years before, when I had asked for help. I still had to be constantly vigilant to stay away from situations that might put me in danger, including those that activated my self-doubt and self-condemnation. Well, I couldn't avoid those feelings now; they went along with the territory of grief. I was to learn that bereaved parents usually feel guilty, no matter how much they have done for their child: nursed her through a terminal illness, anticipated everything, said goodbye. It didn't matter. The feelings weren't entirely rational.

In the following six days, I adapted to the rhythm of the abbey, performing communal jobs like vacuuming or helping in the kitchen. Pema and I spent hours together, talking. I climbed the mountain behind the abbey and burst into tears, feeling furious at Neddy, when I reached the solid, weighty presence of a great rock halfway up the pine-needled trail. My anger at Neddy for not taking care of himself rarely reached the surface; I was more liable to turn the anger inward, to take the blame myself for what had happened, or to blame God.

At other moments there was release from self-condemnation or from rage. The release didn't last very long, however, and the desperate, fearlike feeling came back.

"What can I do for him? SOME thing. SOMETHING."

Then, "Nothing."

Pema taught me to meditate, instructing me to become mindful of the out-breath as it fluttered from my nose. If I found myself losing concentration and musing, agonizing, or reflecting, I should say to myself, "Thinking," in a gentle, accepting way, and then let go of the thought—not to repress it but to realize that it is just thought and not reality—and return to awareness of my breath. As we talked, a fly crawled on Pema's face. She didn't brush it away. The first precept of the abbey was, "no killing."

The meditation room was large and light, with long windows overlooking the sea. Red pads with square red and yellow cushions on top of them lay in rows on the polished floor. The shrine, occupying a central place between the windows, was covered with red and gold cloth. Above it, photographs of holy men surrounded a large scroll of a Buddha.

I tried sitting on a cushion, but my hip hurt from a painful degenerative condition, so, with Pema's permission, I moved to a chair.

Pema left me alone. It took a few minutes to become aware of my breath, to begin to distinguish the in-breath from the out-breath. Simply noticing that air was moving in and out of my lungs —acknowledging my mortality—was extremely frightening. If I could acknowledge that my heart was beating and my lungs were working, then I had to acknowledge that Neddy drew no more breaths into his own lungs, and his heart would never beat again. I sat through the searing pain in my mind that this thought engendered, and gradually I became calmer.

After a few days at the abbey, I began to miss Bill badly. I remembered how he had held me in bed while I sobbed before I left home. I remembered how he hovered supportively at my side as I greeted hundreds of people in the chancel of the church after the funeral. I remembered how much he had loved Neddy, how they joked around together, and teased me.

When we finally spoke on the telephone, however, there wasn't much to say.

I visualized him walking around the apartment, holding his portable phone to his ear. "I looked at a studio in Jersey City," he said, from far away.

Bill had just retired the week before, a huge event in his life. He had been an art teacher in the New York City public school system for thirty-five years, and, even though he felt demeaned by the low pay and difficult conditions, it had been almost impossible to leave. He had been mustering up his courage for a long time. Now that he had made the break, he longed to have his own art studio. He had given up a career as a painter many years ago in order to make enough money to support his family. He had five children in all.

His retirement was completely overshadowed by Neddy's death.

"Oh, good," I said, somewhat facetiously. I was threatened by the idea of the studio, as it signaled a huge change in our relationship. He wanted to live part time in the studio rather than full time with me as he had for almost seven years. I was trying to be understanding, but I felt even more insecure now that Neddy was dead. We were working on these problems and others in couples therapy.

We talked for a short time. When I hung up, I felt exhausted.

I called Martha in San Francisco. She told me she had a cold, and she couldn't help thinking that she might, like Neddy, have a fatal infection.

"Sweetie, it's normal to have those fears," I said, stifling my own swift panic that I might lose her.

"I know."

I thought of how crushed Martha looked three weeks ago when

she entered the apartment where she and Neddy had grown up and lived until they were adults, where I still lived with Bill. I remembered how she had thrown herself into my arms for a long embrace, and how, unable to sleep that night, she had walked out of her room, patted her chest, and said, "My heart is broken."

You were never apart as children. Never apart. She was only twenty-one months older than you were.

In the first days Martha and I sobbed until sobbing seemed as natural as breathing. Strangely, we never cried at the same time. When one of us dried up, the other one would start.

When she left for California, Martha wore Neddy's blue nylon shell, hugging it around her.

Now she cried over the phone.

I meditated every day with the residents of the abbey. To start the meditation, Pema knocked a wooden stave on the lip of a large brass bowl next to her on the small raised platform on which she sat in the lotus position. The resulting clear chime reverberated on and on and on.

In meditation, time crept by, as it would for the next six months until the New Year. Sometimes I felt bored and wondered why I was in this unfamiliar and somewhat uncomfortable place, far away from home. Moods and emotions passed through my mind like clouds passing through the sky. Sometimes I felt dark and rageful, sometimes despairing, sometimes calm and happy. I was accustomed to inhabiting my thoughts; if I feared the future, that was reality; if I regretted the past, that was the truth. Observing, uttering, "Thinking," when I remembered to do it, led me sometimes to a quiet place.

On my last morning at the abbey, I woke up as usual at 4:00 A.M., then went back to sleep until the clacker. Breakfast was hot porridge; hearty, brown, coarse, steaming, and topped with condensed milk; and a bowl of thick, curdy yogurt with fruit. I peeled the labels off my mug and napkin ring, joined the meditation for ten minutes, and then prepared to leave. Pema, as she sat Buddha-like on her platform at the head of the meditation room, met my eyes and raised the first two fingers of her left hand from her knee to signal goodbye.

"You were never apart . . ."

* * *

My brother Phil met my plane later in Bar Harbor, Maine. The trip from Sydney to visit him and his wife Katharine in their summer home had taken seven hours.

"Hi, Dith," Phil greeted me, using my family nickname, and hugged me tightly.

Phil was the second oldest child in the family. First came my big sister Nancy, eleven years older than me; then Phil, ten years older; then my brother Ken, seven years older. Both my brothers and my sister had been at Neddy's funeral.

Phil was our leader, particularly after our parents' deaths. He was our mother's favorite child, her red-haired darling. We looked to him for leadership—and harbored some resentment along the way. But it wasn't easy to hold a grudge or prolong a petty jealousy, because he was a genuinely compassionate and good-hearted man; we all adored him. He and Ken had taught me to throw a perfect spiral pass when I was seven years old—a skill that I still possessed—and helped me to master the art of tackling. I often dressed in full football uniform as a child, and lived the life of a tomboy, in the woods, with a knife at my belt. Phil and Katharine, to whom he had been married for forty years, had always been supportive and kind. We lived an hour apart and Phil and I talked often on the phone. Now I needed to be with him.

It felt like the fifties, when we used to do things together after Phil and Katharine were first married, like going to those batting cages that had automatic pitching machines. Phil would swat 'em like Joltin' Joe. Or we'd visit Asbury Park, spending the evening eating candy corn and cotton candy and riding the Ferris wheel or trying to win a prize at the booths. Or we'd ride the waves at the beach at Mantoloking on the Jersey shore, or fish for trout at Balsam Lake in the Catskills. I just hung out with them; little sister tagging along.

Later, Phil and I went shopping for Bisquick for blueberry muffins. Every few minutes I got my fix: I *had* to bring Neddy up.

But it was so hollow.

I said to God, "Enough already. Stop this joking around. Come *on*. It's time to see him now."

And the realization would hit:

He's dead! He's never coming back! I'll never see his face or hear his voice again!

It was HORRIBLE to have just one child.

The books suggest, when you're asked, to explain that you had two children but that one of them died. Sometimes people conceal the fact that they had another child because it hurts so much to say it.

I slept in a little cabin on the shore of Phil and Katharine's island. The water lapped at the rocks below my window.

It was a beautiful island. It had beaches made of soft ground-up shells, granite ledges, tall pine trees, and three houses: the octagonal main house, just one room ringed with sleeping-couch window seats enclosing a cooking area and a central fireplace; and two sleeping cabins, mine on the shore with a lone pine sticking up through its porch and another in a grassy field at the top of the rise. The island was nine acres in all and was shaped like a narrow sailing vessel, pointing out to the open sea. Phil and Katharine had bought it twenty years ago for $9,000.

I felt so jealous of them for having all of this and six *living* children!

Oh, Neddy. I remember how your little mittens looked, linked together by a long piece of elastic and poking out of your snowsuit sleeves. I remember cutting your hair, delicate fine blond hair—a bowl cut. I remember how you put on your jacket—laying it down on the floor upside down, sticking your arms in the armholes, and whipping it over your head onto your back . . .

At sunrise, I heard the deep, throaty roar of powerful engines as the lobster boats arrived to haul up their pots. I could hear their radios clearly over the water. I got up and looked out the window. A kayaker paddled past the island. The place seemed deserted, but it wasn't.

Crows cawed. A cluster of geese floated by.

A loon took off, leaving little dips in the water with its feet.

Swallows swooped overhead, diving at bugs.

A seagull dropped a sea urchin on the rocks to break it.

I needed someone to say, "You were a wonderful mother." To say, "You did the best you could. Under the circumstances."

Acceptance. Of where and what I'd been.

I was doubting my whole life.

". . . with a lone pine sticking up through its porch."

It seemed as if I had done everything wrong.

Later, I walked down the middle path on the island towards its prow, climbing down to the beach at the starboard side. The tide was coming in, but was still low. I walked forward, stopping to look at beach flowers, seaweed, pink granite rocks, lichen. I felt like I had been cracked like a nut, cracked open for beauty as well as for ugliness and horror, for joy as well as for rage and fear and deep, deep sadness. Eventually I walked around the entire island, hopping from one half-submerged stone to another, favoring my right leg because of pain in my left hip, but intent, examining everything.

Phil, still in his pajamas and with his red-gray hair still mussed up from sleep, made soft-boiled eggs. He tore up a piece of toast and mashed it in with the eggs in the egg cup, added a dollop of butter, mixed everything together, salted it, and gave it to me. Vaguely thinking, *no wonder he had a heart attack,* I obediently ate it all up. Its rich taste reminded me of childhood breakfasts, when cholesterol was unknown.

"Oh, Phil," I said. "I feel so badly. If my divorce hadn't happened, if I had a strong family structure like you do . . ."

"I lucked into that," Phil said, modestly, giving Katharine the credit.

"Well, if I had just called his doctor. I mean, I did call him and then I felt that going behind Neddy's back wasn't a good idea, so I never called back. If I had . . ."

"Hold on," Phil interrupted. "It was Neddy himself who failed to take care of himself. He's the one who broke the doctor's appointment. It wasn't up to you to take care of him anymore. If you did, it would be strange, indeed. Neddy was twenty-seven years old, after all," he emphasized, firmly.

Phil and I talked about the family newsletter he was writing—he was the family historian—and he said he'd added Neddy's death to the news column. I mused, brokenly, about how it just stopped. Neddy's life just stopped. There wouldn't be any more news, ever again.

Phil said, "It's harder on the mother."

I asked, "Why?"

"Because she carried the child inside her; there's that physical connection. No one else can ever feel the loss as you do."

His understanding, his love, had fulfilled a deep need. Now I could go home.

CHAPTER THREE

After returning from Maine at the end of July, I spent the rest of the summer on Long Island in a cottage about a mile from the place where I drank long ago.

Bill and I had rented the same little gray-shingled dwelling for three summers. I had first come to this group of cottages to visit friends years before, and had returned as a guest many times, but it was only when I left my job in publishing to work free lance as a children's book author and illustrator that I was free to be here all summer.

We were lucky to get the cottage, as tenants hardly ever moved out. The layout consisted of a living room/kitchen, bathroom, and two small bedrooms. The floor of the cottage was covered with linoleum; you could sweep the whole place out in minutes. The furnishings were functional: a formica-topped kitchen table, a comfortable sofa and matching armchair covered with black Naugahyde, enough lamps for reading. On the living room wall hung a sampler with a stitched message, TURN ALWAYS TOWARDS THE SUN-SHINE AND SHADOWS WILL ALWAYS FALL BEHIND YOU.

I had appropriated the desk, loading file folders into its drawer along with pencils, pens, a pair of scissors, masking tape, a magnifying glass, stamps, scratch pads, rubber bands, paper clips, envelopes. Also packed into the cottage were my light box, drawing pencils, watercolor set, acrylic paints and brushes, a slide projector, laptop computer, printer, cameras and lenses, and drawing pads. On the extra beds in the spare bedroom I piled the books I planned to read for research. Bill accused me of leaving no room for him. I justified myself for hogging the space because he was there less time—only two months out of four—and he didn't have as much stuff. One summer he painted outside the cottage, leaning a canvas up against the shingles, but the sun was too hot and the wind blew his equipment around. Another summer he painted in someone's toolshed. We had a hard time living together in the small space, especially since we had very different habits: he liked to listen to radio talk shows and do a lot of talking himself, and I liked silence.

When I returned from Maine, Bill was withdrawn and withholding. I felt scorned. I just wanted him to love me, but he was drifting farther and farther away.

Looking back, I think Bill probably felt that my grief threatened his dream of being an artist. Probably he thought he would have to drop everything and take care of me, now that I was wounded. Being around me probably made him feel guilty and angry all the time. Our grief about Neddy separated us further. I was trying for once in my life to not run away from feelings, to not push them down, to allow myself to cry and mourn and vent my rage. Bill accused me of "braying," and could hardly stand being around me. Later I read in grief books about how men and women express grief in different ways.

As the summer progressed, we saw each other less and less. Mostly, Bill stayed in the city and I lived out on Long Island. We talked on the phone. When Bill did come out for the weekend or I went into the city, we were delighted to see each other at first but within moments started squabbling.

Then Bill terminated couples therapy. He had found an artist's studio in Staten Island. He told me that it was a railroad flat in an inexpensive neighborhood, and that he could see the Hudson River and the Verrazano Narrows Bridge from the window, but he didn't invite me to visit.

Bill helped me to delude myself. Even though he planned to live in his studio, at least for a while, he was still paying part of the monthly maintenance fees for my apartment. I assumed that we would still see each other, visiting each other's apartments, still sleeping together, when I returned to the city at the end of the summer, and he didn't disabuse me of that notion.

Meanwhile, I was glad to be on Long Island. Every day I bicycled around what I called "my square." This was a four-mile stretch of roads enclosing a square area of the most beautiful farmland left on Long Island. Even though my hip and lower back hurt when I biked, this ride was an important ritual for me, and exercise was essential to ease the turmoil in my head.

I rode out of the driveway, turned left, and breathed a sigh of relief as I left the sheltering trees. Barely twenty yards from the end of the driveway, fields planted with rye, potatoes, and corn stretched almost to the sea two miles away, and the great arc of the sky extended from horizon to horizon. Farther down the road, I passed a big house that had been built backwards; that is, the owners first constructed the extensive gardens and later the house was erected among them. I turned left on Bridge Lane and glided through a tunnel of trees to the rustic two-lane bridge which spanned a pond. This was my favorite place on the square. The bridge was a popular spot in summer; clusters of people with nets on long poles fished for blue crabs, using chicken necks for bait. At sunset, children and parents fished for sunnies from the concrete abutment of the bridge. Once, as I rode by, a large woman heaved a squirming eel up from the water and straight back over her shoulder, almost splatting me in the face. Often I paused on the crown of the bridge to fill my lungs and then gaze north and then south at the reed-lined shore. There was something special about the luminous quality of the light here. I frequently arrived before sunrise to watch egrets wade in the shallows, and sometimes I stayed on in the evening until darkness fell.

Leaving the bridge behind, I continued on my route. Hammering announced the construction of a new house across the road. A potato field had been sold off, and homes were going up. The land inside the square could not be sold, as it was to be preserved in a special trust that benefited farmers if they kept it in cultivation, which was one way that the county was trying to retain the rural character of this area.

I made a detour at the end of the second leg in the square, riding out the straight road to the beach. I had to check out the height of the waves and their set, measure the strength of the wind, view the cloud conditions. Often a pickup truck was parked on the sand at the entrance to the beach, and its driver was doing the same thing I was: taking a reading, so to speak, of the day.

The third leg of the square led me past an eighteenth-century burying ground with worn, askew stones, past a horse farm, past a working greenhouse and white clapboard houses surrounded with privet hedges, to the small general store and post office. Deliberately old-fashioned in looks and character, the store sold newspapers and sandwiches, and ran a thriving catering business. I bought the paper with money already counted out in the pocket of my shorts, and picked up my mail from the postmaster. After stowing the newspaper in my bike basket, I pedaled over the uneven paving stones of a sidewalk, ducking hanging leaves, and made my left turn at a one-room schoolhouse, pedaling faster now on this busier road. After I passed a parsonage built in 1730, I turned left again and coasted into my driveway.

Here you rode your bike to see your friends. Here you fed me strawberries as I drove the car; you went to the general store; you climbed that tree; we played catch here outside the cottages.

Sometimes I imagine holding you on my lap, your little-boy body squirming, your red-sneakered feet drumming on my legs. Other days you seem irretrievably gone. Will I see you again when I die? Will my life just be a lingering until that moment of release?

The anger you feel when you lose someone you love, particularly when they are torn away from you too soon, is so powerful and terrifying that you may not even know that what you are feeling, that the burning inside you is anger. One day, while crossing the street in a nearby town, I wanted to grab a police officer's revolver out of his holster and shoot someone.

Who would I shoot? I didn't know.

I started to park my bike at the beach and walk to the ocean's edge every morning. There I picked up sticks and stones and other debris, and, screaming, hurled them into the sea. A friend who had AIDS had offered, "If you want me to start you off, I'll be happy to." I was too shy to scream in front of him, so I did it alone. After about a week, I was so hoarse I had to stop. The idea remained; it was O.K. to feel angry.

Martha seemed to know what to do with her anger without any coaching. She called one day to tell me that she had screamed in her car all the way out to a workshop in Mill Valley. Later she went alone to Mount Tamalpais and climbed her favorite trail, where she screamed and cried.

As far as I could tell, both Martha and I were in the second stage of grief. It might take two years or more to complete the five-stage process of grief and mourning, I would learn. First, there is shock and denial that what has happened is, in fact, true; then confusion and turmoil lead to a sense of disorganization; the third stage is a feeling of intense despair; followed by acute loneliness; and, finally, relief and reconnection to life. If one postpones some or all of these stages, they may crop up inappropriately in later years.

I spoke to Elizabeth, Neddy's girlfriend at the time of his death. She was in a hyperactive state, filling up her time with restless activity in an attempt to blot out the pain.

"I picture Ned in two ways; with that incredible smile and ready to hug me when I came home at night, and when he was so sick the day before he died.

"His death is unacceptable. I just want another day with him, or an hour. I remember when you wrote him that letter saying I was in denial about his illness. I just had no exposure to illness. It was ignorance, not denial. I'm so sorry. I'm so sorry."

Her words reminded me how powerful a force denial had been in my life and I saw even more clearly how it affected Neddy as well. Living with a heart ailment can bring denial, and Neddy so desperately wanted to believe there was nothing wrong with him.

In another conversation Elizabeth told me of their plans together. "He was going to stay at the bank for five years, then we both planned to move away. I'm going to move away from New Jersey now. I'm determined to use my resources and go on."

"Isak Dinesen said any sorrow can be borne if you put it in a story," she added, when she heard about my journal.

*   *   *

One day I got a call from a local minister offering help, so I bicycled up to the church. Bob described a pamphlet about prayer that he wanted me to read.

"You've got to ask God for what you want."

"What I want! What I want! I want my son back!" I burst out bitterly, furiously. I told him about the "what ifs" and the "I should have's" and how I screamed at the sea.

"Good! Tell God you're angry! He can handle it." Bob clasped my hand in both of his and asked God to help me come before Him real. "Your prayers should be 'I don't know why you did this! I'm angry at you!' "

Later, I biked to the bay. A small meditation group run by members of Bob's church met beside the lapping waves. We addressed God, "You have sustained us through the darkness; and you bless us with life in this new day. In the shadow of your wings we sing for joy and bless your holy name."

Pema's method of meditation was new to me, but meditation itself wasn't. My first introduction to it had been in the seventies, when I learned Transcendental Meditation. After a year, unable to keep up the discipline of sitting twice a day for twenty minutes while repeating a mantra, I let the TM slide. During the eighties, I maintained a ritual of reading spiritual literature in the morning and setting aside a time of reflection before my morning prayers. Sometimes the period of reflection was very short: a few seconds or minutes. When I became a jogger, I consciously used the pounding of my feet on the pavement to propel me into a meditative state. Around the time of Neddy's heart operation, I took a course on meditation that helped me to sit still long enough to recognize my feelings, which were often bottled up and hidden, even from myself.

I was a member of a second meditation group which met in a chapel overlooking a pond. Late in the summer, geese often glided, honking, over the chapel, coasting in to land on the water. This second meditation group was dedicated to the concept of seeking conscious contact with God—however one wished to interpret God—through prayer and meditation, praying only for knowledge of his will for us, and the power to carry that out.

One morning during meditation I imagined myself floating up to the top of the chapel in a kind of radiant light that filled the ceiling. I twirled in the light as I hung there, like a sea otter rolling in long strands of kelp, anchored and safe for the night. Later, in Neddy's memory, I wrote the outline of a children's story about a sea otter.

Meditation didn't mitigate my rage, although it helped me see it more clearly. I was angry at Neddy, and sometimes I couldn't even look at the photographs of him I'd propped up on my bureau. At other times I pored over them.

I was also enraged with Neddy's doctors. Early in the grieving process I had realized that I had a choice: I could go the route of hating the doctors, or one of them in particular, blaming him (for I genuinely thought that he had let Neddy down), but that was just another way of avoiding the central fact of Neddy's death, and would simply postpone facing the feelings I would sooner or later have to endure.

Neddy's internist, Dr. K, who was a friend, had phoned two days after the funeral. "I just got back from vacation, Edith, and I'm terribly, terribly sorry," he said.

Believing that he had missed the fact that Neddy was as sick as he was, I couldn't believe Jim had the gall to call. "I . . . I can't talk to you, Jim," I stuttered, and hung up.

But then I prayed: *"Dear God, help me. I can't afford to walk around with a resentment at anyone."*

I dialed his number. The receptionist put me right through. "I'm glad you called back, Edith," Jim said. "We saw it coming," he stated, and then repeated, "We saw it coming. He was very sick but we didn't know why."

I said, "I'm very angry at you, Jim, and I'm really furious at Dr. G, for letting him drive all that way with chest pains."

Jim sighed and said, "I'm not going to justify myself to you, Edith." But then he added, "I suspected a heart infection and did a sedimentation rate and a urine and a blood count. Usually with this kind of infection the sed rate is up and the blood count is down and the urine is bloody, and none of these things were true. But we're not even sure it was this kind of infection, because there was no post-mortem."

I said, "I wanted a post-mortem, but Neddy's father didn't."

"If I'd been there I would have definitely recommended it," Jim stated.

"Well, Dr. G said if it were his child he wouldn't have a post-mortem," I said.

"Oh, dear. I would have recommended it," said Jim.

The morning after this conversation, sometime before dawn, I lay on the floor of my bedroom in the cottage, moaning, rocking, and almost but not quite banging my head on the floor. Just sort of bumping it.

Later I pulled myself up from the floor and began to read Stephen Levine's book, *Healing Into Life and Death.* Levine had worked with the dying and those that mourn them for many years. He was the author of several books on the subject of spiritual healing and a teacher of Buddhist-based principles. In this particular book, he wrote that often resistance to feelings is the cause of one's suffering, not the feelings themselves. If one can begin to soften the resistance to sadness, rage, or even physical pain, if one can begin to examine the resistance itself, even for a second at a time, something changes. The pain "begins to melt in the mind." Letting down one's resistance is incredibly difficult to do, as one automatically tries to protect oneself from the feelings, but Levine suggests gently pressing on a point which he calls the grief point in the center of the sternum. "Breathe the pain into your heart. Let in the grief of a lifetime . . ."

Slowing down and feeling the pain was the most important lesson I learned about grieving. Now I knew why I had chosen to stay alone on Long Island.

CHAPTER FOUR

In August, I went to a meeting of The Compassionate Friends, a grief group for bereaved parents. There were nine people at the meeting, including a couple whose young daughter had died that week. Her stomach had exploded—something I couldn't even begin to contemplate. The couple were born-again Christians and had a very, very strong belief. They wouldn't allow themselves to be angry at God. The wife said she believed each person on Earth has a job, and when that job is done, he or she simply leaves. I cried when she said this. She said she kept moving, never stopping, from morning to night, to get away from the pain.

An older Hispanic woman's thirty-seven-year-old son had died of liver cancer. He was in agony at the end and couldn't speak, but signaled that he wanted hugs and kisses. She climbed into the hospital bed and held him. She still went several times a day to the cemetery. At home she talked out loud to her son, wishing him good night and good morning. His dog still sat by his chair.

The group leader had lost her own son in a car accident. Another woman's daughter had committed suicide with no warning— she wasn't even depressed. Another's sixteen-year-old son was driving home one night and his pickup truck overturned. He was killed just a half mile from their house. Another child was hit by a car. Another died of a cocaine overdose.

Each of us told of our children's deaths. Unlike myself, the others were fairly aggressive about speaking up. I wondered if this was their only forum, which wasn't true about me. I saw friends, spoke up, and got hugs at my recovery support group every day. Here, I felt a little left out.

After a coffee break, the members of the grief group started talking about a psychic they had all been to. One woman thought he was a swindler. The others said he helped them. The woman whose son had died of the cocaine overdose said she didn't even care if the guy *was* a fake; she hadn't gotten closure in the whole five years since her son died, until she heard "him" speak through the lips of the psychic. "He" told her it was an accidental overdose, not purposeful, which helped her to let go.

I found grief groups helpful in that they brought me into contact with other bereaved parents. I discovered I had a ghoulish interest in tragedies I considered "worse" than Neddy's: murders, terrible accidents, suicides. Somehow it was reassuring to see the parents walking, talking, living in the world, carrying on. I learned that grief sometimes worsens after six months and at a year; that anger at doctors is very common; that most parents have difficulty cleaning out their dead child's room; some have problems with handling other people's reactions to the death; some have fears that their children are cold, or hungry in their graves. One woman in the group put a nightlight in her son's coffin, another a blanket. Another preserved her son's dirty laundry.

The group met only once a month, which was its main drawback. However, connections were made, telephone numbers were exchanged, and support was offered.

One woman in the group was taking sleeping pills to dull the pain. I knew that sleeping pills or tranquilizers would set off my addictive nature and lead me back to drinking. Surprisingly, I never felt like drinking during the whole mourning period—which pointed to the miraculous nature of recovery.

After a month or so at the beach, my energy began to come back in bursts. One day I caught sight of a huge flock of geese in the field near my cottage. I changed into long pants and high socks which I pulled up over the cuffs of the pants to keep out ticks, put my 80–200 mm lens on my camera, cleaned the lens with antistatic cloth, and crept through the high weeds at the end of the corn patch to the macadam road that ran along the edge of the field.

The geese were just beginning to edge my way because a farmer was climbing onto his tractor, which was parked at the other end of the field, but they reversed direction when I stepped into the ruts and began to walk toward them. Eventually clusters and then a whole cloud of them took off and flew toward the pond.

". . . a whole cloud of them took off . . ."

I had taken a roll of film quickly so I returned home, changed films and lenses and biked to the bridge, where I photographed some crabs that a scrawny, grizzled man had caught. When I said I wanted to photograph him, he assented, nervously, "Awright, as long as I don't end up in jail!"

Grief would hit out of the blue and when I least expected it: one day I turned on the radio and heard a report about Buddy Harrelson, who was currently the manager of the Mets. Immediately I felt agonizing sadness, for Buddy had been part of the Amazin' Mets who won the pennant in 1973. Neddy and I knew them all:

Tom Seaver, Buddy, Jerry Koosman, Rusty Staub, and Neddy knew all their stats. Later, when the Mets were in the World Series again, I watched every game and called Neddy in New Jersey for a rehash afterwards.

Biking to the bay, I thought again of Neddy's body in the hospital, his open mouth, his eyes stationary and staring in different directions through slits of lids, and started to sob. I needed to fixate on such a terrible image because I had to know that Neddy was dead. That was my work right now, knowing he was dead.

Martha traveled east again from California in the second week of September. I met her at the airport and drove her to Long Island. It was wonderful to see her. She looked a lot like me, with her short brown hair, except that she was about 5′5″, a couple of inches shorter than I was, and had one long, thin pigtail reaching down to her waist and three earrings dangling from her right earlobe. I thought about the first time I had ever seen her after she was born, and I fell in love with her. I remembered how she nuzzled into my breast when she drank my milk, and, older, lying in her crib, contemplated her fist, and her throaty giggles when I played peek-a-boo and blew noisy air against her velvety soft stomach . . . Now she sat beside me in the cottage as I sobbed, her arm around my shoulders. She murmured, "None of your loving went to waste. His life was meaningful."

The weather had turned sharply colder. When I biked in the morning, I wore my turquoise Day-Glo glove liners, blue jeans, and a windbreaker over a sweater. The bridge was deserted for the first time all summer.

Martha drove into the city and brought back all of the negatives for all of the photographs I'd ever taken in the last thirty years, four huge shopping bags stuffed full. She was consumed with the need to make a record of Neddy's life. She studied the negatives on my light box, searching out her favorites. Martha complained, poignantly, "I was looking forward to middle age and old age with him. Now I don't have anyone to say, 'Remember this? Remember that?' to."

The seasons were changing. Autumn was approaching. The sunlight had lost its summer harshness and the days were growing shorter. A sign reading, LEMONADE 25 CENTS, written in a childish hand, lay crumpled and discarded by the road to the beach. Goldenrod and Queen Anne's lace filled the uncultivated fields, while delicate new shoots of mint-green winter rye pushed their way up in some of the plowed fields.

It was potato-digging time. The leaves of the potato plants had withered, leaving the tubers to ripen underground. I watched a potato-digging machine clank its way through the furrows. The machine scooped up dirt, withered leaves, roots, and potatoes and dumped them on a conveyor belt. The roots, leaves, and dirt fell away from the heavier potatoes, which climbed up the belt until they plunged off into a trough, then rolled down it and spilled onto another belt, which carried them the length of the machine and then at right angles onto an arm from which they spilled into a truck which was being driven parallel to the digger. The truck, a sturdy World War II model, had high wooden sides to hold the potatoes in. The driver varied his speed so that the potatoes piled up evenly from front to back. All the while, barn swallows flitted and swooped around the vehicles or seemed to hang motionless in the air. They were feasting on bugs that were being stirred up from the field.

Martha and I drove to the beach to get warm, since there was no heat in the cottage. Exhausted, we lay down near the dunes. The sand was hot, and Martha went to sleep on her side. I was bitten through my sock by a blackfly, so I got up and strolled down to the water.

With a jolt, I realized that the water was boiling with fish. Bluefish rushed and flopped and flapped to feed in a frenzy on tiny silver minnows. The water was choppy with bluefish tails and fins and heads poking up and slapping and disappearing. There was a chattering sound from the splashing. The little minnows were so thick that the water was brown with them. Thousands of them washed up with the waves and were left, a glittering residue of arching tiny bodies, trying to get back to the sea.

Surf fishermen in hip boots flung their catch high up on the sand. The big fishes arched and fought, too, and tumbled down the incline toward the water. A few well-placed kicks sent them flying farther from the flapping sea.

A dog, a black Labrador, was swimming in the surf, and, attracted by the leaping fray, swam over to take a look. I was frightened for him, as the frenzied fish were vicious biters. I envisioned the dog stripped of its meat as if by piranhas, a swimming skeleton.

Martha went into the city. That night I finally talked on the telephone to Dr. G, Neddy's cardiologist, who had repeatedly refused to meet with me in person and with whom I'd been trying to arrange a phone conversation for a month.

First I asked, "What happened?"

"What do you mean?" Dr. G answered. "I told you what happened the night he passed on."

"How long had he had the infection?"

"I'm sorry, but I can't answer your question. It would be pure speculation," Dr. G stated, firmly.

"Was it his second job that got him so run-down that the bacteria could get in?"

"I can't answer your question."

"What?" *Why not?*

"Why are you asking me these questions?"

"To get some sense of closure." *You'll never know how frightened I've been about this conversation. To hear the details hurts so very, very much . . .*

"I understand, Mrs. Davis."

"Why did you say Neddy could run a marathon when his friends were saying he looked like he had AIDS?"

"I *didn't* say he could run a marathon. He looked well to me the last time I saw him, but not *that* well. I said, 'I'm glad that you *feel* well enough to run a marathon, Ned, but it would not be good for you to do so.' "

Neddy told me you said he was as "healthy as a horse," even though he'd lost weight and had that terrible cough. He said you said he could train for the marathon. When I told Dr. K about it at the time, he responded that he completely disagreed with you about the marathon. He was going to call you about it, but I can't make myself say all this out loud . . .

Later I learned that Neddy misinterpreted Dr. G's advice because Dr. G had not completely forbidden running.

"Martha had some questions. She wanted to know, did he say anything before he died? Did he know he was going to die? Was he in pain? Was he scared?"

"No, he did not know he was dying." *How do you know?*

The doctor continued. "He wasn't scared." *But he told his stepmother in the hospital that he was scared. And he asked the nurse if he was dying.*

"He seemed comfortable. I don't think anybody thinks they're dying." *Huh? What about all the people Elizabeth Kubler-Ross helps?*

I gathered my courage and inquired, "Why did Dr. K say, 'We saw it coming but we didn't know what it was?' "

"I think you should talk to Jim about that."

"Did you know Neddy was looking for a local doctor in New Jersey? He was so worried! Oh, and the cough. He had it since January. Wasn't it a clue to his condition?"

"I can't answer your question."

Isn't he going to answer anything? "Martha and I wanted to talk to the nurse who was there that night. But it doesn't really matter, anymore." *I'm really angry now. What's the use? What's the point?*

I decided to try one last question. I *knew* he wouldn't answer this one! "You probably won't answer this, either, but why did you tell Neddy to drive thirty miles to the city when he had chest pains? There was a hospital half a mile from his house."

"I think you *know* why I can't answer *that*. Your son was a very strong person. Why did he do a lot of things that he did?"

There was a long silence.

"I guess that's all," I muttered, bitterly.

A longer silence stretched on and on.

"I hope you get some closure," Dr. G said, finally.

"I'm very angry, and not just at you. At the whole thing. That he's dead."

"I understand. And I have a great deal of sympathy for you and for your family," he said, in a strained voice. I remembered that he had cared a lot about Neddy.

"Well. I guess that's all," I repeated absently. *I don't want to hang up because it will sever this link with Neddy.*

"I hope I've been able to bring you some comfort," the doctor muttered.

"Well, goodbye," I rejoined, coldly.

"Goodbye."

After the conversation, I was consumed with anger.

I felt like hanging myself.

Oh, God. He could be alive.

How could this happen?

SHIT.

In the long run it doesn't matter if they screwed up, the doctors.

Dear God, I want to slash my wrists.

Later, I read the Book of Common Prayer, "Lord Jesus Christ, Good shepherd of the sheep, you gather the lambs in your arms and carry them in your bosom: We commend to your loving care this child. Relieve his pain, guard him from all danger, restore him to your gifts of gladness and strength . . ."

In the midst of life we are in death;
Of whom may we seek for succor,
but of Thee, O Lord . . .

"I know that my redeemer liveth, and that he shall stand at the latter day upon the earth: and though this body be destroyed, yet shall I see God; whom I shall see for myself and mine eyes shall behold, and not as a stranger."

"Let the pain in."

The face of that starving woman on Madison Avenue. Her filthy raincoat, her raglike shoes. That face that is always the same, and from which I hide my eyes. Let it in.

The face of the young minister at church last year. A dying face. And, in that case, a serene one. The face of AIDS.

The face of Dad as he hobbled on his crutches.

Press into the chest.

Press into the pain of the heart.

Go past the grief—past it, past it, opening to the light—a tunnel. "Fear and loss suspended in compassionate mercy."

Now I was that bushy-faced otter, rolling over and over in the light.

Blissfully.
Coated with light.

At sunrise, cycling, I was aware of the whole huge breadth of the Earth turning away to the east. Geese took off from the pond as I crossed the bridge, six of them, and flew north, crossing the blood-red sun.

I showered, ate breakfast, sat in my big white robe on my bed with pale sunlight patched on the bedspread, listening to Bach's Toccata and Fugue in D Minor, and began to feel a little better.

The last straw came a few days later:

"Hi," Bill said before he even heard my voice on the phone.

"I don't want you at Neddy's burial! How can you think you can stand by his grave when you're fucking someone else?" I spat out, without any preamble.

"I'm not," he said. "Well, if it makes it easier for you to think it's another woman . . ."

"What do you mean?" I asked. "Isn't there another woman? You told me there was yesterday."

"We're just good friends," he said.

"This is really confusing. You lied to me. You said we were still in an exclusive relationship but you lied to me."

"I didn't but . . ."

"Take the rest of your fucking stuff out of the apartment and leave your key with the doorman," I said, and then started crying and crying and crying.

"Oh, Edith," he said, in a sweet voice.

I sobbed and sobbed. I was totally out of control.

"This may be crazy," I snuffled, "but I still want you to go with us to the burial."

"That *is* crazy. Martha can drive you, can't she?"

"I already rented a car," I mumbled.

"Oh."

"Yeah. I *thought* you might not show up!"

"At least you're mad at me," Bill said. "That's good."

"It's your same old pattern. You just go from one relationship to another. You'll never be alone and grow up!" I exclaimed.

A moment later, I said, "Well, goodbye!" and slammed down the phone.

That night I experienced the worst despair of my life.

I visualized Bill's possessions; his Alice in Wonderland painting, his messy bureau, his nude painting of me—where were they now? Where were his sweaters? Shirts? It was just like Neddy. I had to sort through each piece of clothing, each memory.

No! I didn't want to do it! It wasn't fair!

I beat the bed with a belt, yelling, "Fuck you! Fuck you! Fuck you, Bill!"

I don't care if 70 percent of all marriages and relationships break up after a child's death!

Oh, shit. Why can't I let go? It wasn't right in so many ways. It hasn't been right for two years. Two years out of seven.

I was crying, curled up, begging, "Mummy, Daddy. Please. Come back. Come back and help me."

It was the worst night of my life.

And yet, when I got up in the morning, it was the most beautiful day of the summer.

I changed the bed, took a shower, hung out the rugs, vacuumed with Neddy's Dustbuster, ate breakfast, watched the news, and rode on my bicycle to the store for the paper.

I prayed, too.

Dear God, Thy will be done.

Later, I went down to the ocean. The beach was deserted, empty of summer crowds. I sat on a little cliff the waves had made and contemplated the water.

Staring. Staring. Staring. Out at the sea.

Suddenly, a black object crossed my field of vision. I focused in time to see a big tail slide into the waves, about a hundred yards out. Then came the spout—a puff, quickly dissipating. A whale! The animal surfaced, dove and blew again, and then once more. I could tell by its shape that it was a humpback. Later, when I asked, lifetime residents of this area had never seen a whale here or anywhere near here.

The day before, I had been reading a letter Neddy had sent me on a trip I'd taken to Baja California to watch whales. I guess I didn't pay enough attention to the letter. After I saw the whale, though, I went home and read it again.

" —a puff, quickly dissipating."

On the back of the envelope Neddy had written, "Here is one *whale* of a letter. Ha Ha Ha!!!"

Inside the envelope part of his letter read, "Now, if *I* were on that whale watching trip think about how much *you* would be worrying. You would go crazy! But since *you* are on the trip *I* will have to worry. God, a whale could knock your boat over, or you could drown, or you could get caught in a gale. I mean, all kinds of amazingly disastrous things could happen. But if they did what could I do? Absolutely nothing. So I do not worry. Just like when I am at a friend's house or learning to drive. Bad things could really happen but there is absolutely nothing you could do to prevent it, so don't worry!"

Who else but God could deliver a sign in the form of a whale?

CHAPTER FIVE

Near the end of September, Martha and I drove into the city from Long Island through the Midtown Tunnel and threaded our way through the streets to my ex-husband's apartment building. Martha ran in and got Neddy's ashes. The doorman handed them to her in a stapled-together shopping bag. We drove home, and Martha took them upstairs to the apartment while I parked the car.

The ashes were in a cylindrical silver can, about a foot and a half tall, with an indented top. A white label read, "This temporary receptacle contains the cremated remains of

EDWARD DAVIS
NEW YORK, NEW YORK
NO: 15349

For perpetual security a permanent urn and niche should be provided.

TRINITY CHURCH CREMATORY
770 RIVERSIDE DRIVE
NEW YORK, N.Y. 10032
COLUMBARIUM * NICHES * URNS * CHAPEL

The canister was heavy, surprisingly heavy. I carried it into the bathroom—with both hands—to weigh it on the bathroom scale.

God. It would be awful if I dropped it and the top came off. But I guess that won't happen. A friend told me they needed a can opener to open her mother-in-law's canister before scattering them.

The canister weighed 8.5 pounds.

Having the ashes and holding them didn't feel particularly creepy, or particularly comforting.

I took the canister into Neddy's old bedroom and placed it on the floor where his double-decker bed used to be. I sat down next to the canister.

Neddy, I want to be reverent to you, to respect you.

What could I do that would violate your dignity?

I suppose if I ate the ashes, but there would be nothing wrong with that.

Ingested them.

A memory of carrying you inside; how you kicked, a restless, boyish kick, unlike sweet Martha, who bumped in a softer way.

I pulled the canister between my thighs and crooked my legs around it.

I wish I could birth you all over again, start anew.

Did you finish what you had to do on earth? Will you be born again? Will I?

Oh, my baby. I held you in my arms. You suckled at my breast. Pulled on the teat. Fell asleep with your mouth all milky against my skin.

Your changing table was here, and your crib over there, and before that, your bassinet with its blue satin bows.

Your little newborn body was so long, so long-waisted.

The little puckered pouch, and your little penis. When you peed you'd hit the wall sometimes, depending on the angle.

You got diarrhea, from my drinking gin.

I hate to remember that.

One time, when you were older, you smeared shit all over your crib and on the wall.

Did I spank you then? I never should have spanked you. Your father used to do it too. No one ever spanked me.

You were a spunky boy. Not a doormat.

You were hyper.

You put the block in your training pants so I would hurt my hand when I whacked you.

Oh, why did I do it?

That time when you were about eight years old and you grabbed the knife. You were in trouble. And I took you to be shrunk, and I took myself. The shrink said, "Give him love," and I did. You lapped it up, like a desert laps up water. I was very sick but I'm glad I could respond even then. Oh, God, why, why? I wasn't a perfect mother by any means. I was sick. I'm sorry. I'm so horribly sorry.

I drank and smoked when I was pregnant and if that's how you got the deformation in your heart, what can I say? That no one warned me? That they didn't know then what they know now? Anyway, your father has a heart murmur. I can't take credit for that. But I'm sorry. I'm sorry I was the way I was, a sick alcoholic. I haven't been that way for seventeen years.

I leaned back against a tall built-in bookcase that reached almost to the ceiling. When he was small, Neddy used to climb up to the top shelf and leap across to the upper deck of his double-decker bed.

He organized his books by subject matter. Coin collecting. History. Fiction. *To Kill a Mockingbird, Chitty Chitty Bang Bang, Charlie and the Glass Elevator, Homer Price.*

In the little bathroom off the bedroom, the hooks for hanging up his snowsuit by its hood were still there. *Your mittens, attached to each other by a long piece of elastic, poked out the sleeves.*

I tried to warm the canister with my hand, sobbed.

You always felt I loved Martha more, because she had the bigger room.

It isn't true. She just lucked out because she was born first.

Your bed was over there. You designed it yourself. The bottom deck was a formica desktop supported by two bureaus, and the upper deck was a bed. You and your father built it together.

I used to climb up, using the desk as a step because there was no ladder, to give you back rubs. Great kneadings of the shoulder muscles, rubbings of the spine.

Bill used to store his art supplies in this room. Now it was empty.

You loved Bill and welcomed him. "A magician," you called him. He brought, you said, happiness into my life as never before. That was a generous thing to say, Neddy. A very generous thing.

* * *

Although this monologue was infinitely painful, it was an important ritual I knew I must invent and endure. I wanted the ashes to physically be in each room of the apartment, where Neddy had lived for twenty-four years, and in each one I would address him. Now I took the canister into Martha's room, set it on the floor, said a few words, and left it there while I lay down on my bed for a restless catnap.

Later, I carried the canister into the living room. The windows looked out on the street. Bars to keep the children from falling out were still in place. Transparent stickers that Martha and Neddy had put there were still pasted on a windowpane, just kid-high. The piano, where the children labored on sharps and flats, stood near the windows. A painting I had done of Neddy with his bike hung over the fireplace, as it had for twenty years. Neddy's *The Next Whole Earth Catalog* was still in the bookcase, as were the children's books that I used to read out loud: *Ping, The Fox Went Out on a Chilly Night, Madeline.*

Everything reminded me of Neddy, even the big green rug, where he had set up his orange Hot Wheels track. I talked to him and told him all about the room and my memories, as if he were a blind man and couldn't see.

Then I carried the ashes into my bedroom. A high shelf in the bookcase behind the door held a dusty display of Neddy's and Martha's artwork from grammar school. Neddy had fashioned a dog out of wire, and had made, painted, and glazed numerous clay objects: an elephant with floppy ears and a flattish, funny-looking trunk; a clay baseball bank, painted white, with a slot for money; a clay ashtray with a clay cigarette resting in it; and a clay emperor penguin. Pinned up at the back of the shelf were several of Neddy's drawings of racing cars: pink, elongated, surreal. Lodged between the elephant and the bank I found a Super Ball, a small ball made of compacted material streaked with spiraling variegated colors, which must have been lying there for about fifteen years. It still bounced just fine.

On my bureau lay half a clamshell with a rock glued into its valve. It looked like a soap dish. On the rock was written SOAP, in Neddy's childish hand. Next to it was the glass bear that I had

*"You and Martha
wrapped in the towel."*

given him for graduation from college, retrieved from his bureau
in New Jersey after he died. Propped against the bear was a note
Neddy had sent from camp:

"Dear Mummy: i got hear safely and i will write you later by
(sic) love Neddy."

I told him about the photographs on the bureau: *You and me
and Martha in Ireland. You in front of the fireplace. You hugging
Martha. You and Martha wrapped in the towel. You in your soccer
uniform. You as a tiny boy with the yellow beach ball.*

On a shelf near the bathroom was a shiny black and gold plaque
with a molded plastic baseball, complete with seam, protruding
from it. The inscription read, CHAMPIONS BASEBALL MVP 1972 NED DA-
VIS.

I carried the canister into the kitchen and set it on the yellow tin-topped table. Neddy's seat was in the corner, Martha's facing him. He always used a bright pink plastic plate. Martha had a white plate with blue flowers.

Oh, Neddy. You used to love potato skins, with lots of butter. And hot dogs. You sat right here.

My dear boy. I don't want to stop talking to you.

But I guess I've got the rest of my life to do that, if I want to.

Except that the burial of the ashes has to be some kind of closure. Your hair consumed by fire. Your toes. Your fingernails. Your heart. Oh, God. Help me.

You didn't want your body to rot.

"Reduced to my carbon."

This is what you wanted.

God, take care of him. Rock him and hold him, as I did.

Oh, Neddy, I would die for you.

But that would be stupid.

It's better to live. For myself.

All these words, which I feel are so important, don't mean anything. What's the point? You're dead. You can't hear me. But I suppose I'm trying to let go. I have to let go.

CHAPTER SIX

Martha drove me up to the graveyard in Brookfield, Connecticut, near where her grandparents once had a farm, where we had also formerly had a house.

I feel so stupidly self-conscious. Will I faint? Will I fall in the grave? Will I cry? Or, worse yet, will I do nothing, tough it out?

We looked for familiar landmarks along the way: the pink roadside dinosaur, the fairgrounds, but they were gone.

A new part of the highway bisected what used to be the farm and we traveled past cliffs formed by blasting. Turning off the highway, we drove onto our old road. It was more populated than it had been twenty years ago. As we neared the border of the farm, we saw a big post office on the left and a municipal center on the right, where there used to be fields. A firehouse was also under construction. The United Parcel Service building, the first commercial structure built on the road after the land was sold, marked the old property line of the farm. After UPS, there were nondescript small factories: a leather company, something called Stuter, and Integrity Tile Co. & Ceramics. They were undistinguished grayish buildings. There was no hint anymore of the 100-acre farm, or of my in-laws' two houses, or of our house, or the barn or the chicken coop or the cutting garden or the shop or the tennis court or my mother-in-law's little writing house, or any landmark or tree or curve or driveway that was familiar from ten years of living there.

We drove farther, down to the end of the road, bewildered and sad. We passed under the railroad bridge and rounded a corner. Suddenly the road was totally familiar. Martha burst out, "Isn't this the way to the Pumple Bridge?" and I remembered the wooden bridge that made a noise, "Pumple, pumple," as you drove over it.

"Yes."

Turning around, we retraced our path. Finally, I saw something familiar: a stretch of trees between the Integrity Tile Co. and Stuter.

We drove into the Stuter driveway and parked in a big parking lot. From there we could see the highway and the new cliff at its farther side. I imagined the row of apple trees leading out from my in-laws' house to the swimming pool, which had been located just about where we stood now. I imagined our own house next door and the little green playhouse, peaked-roofed and open-sided like a pagoda, that Ned had built in the field near it. The little green house was called the Cowboy House, because Martha and Neddy used to play cowboy there and wear their chaps and pretend to cook with miniature tin cookware. I walked to the edge of the grass bordering the parking lot and saw some purple asters with yellow centers growing in the weeds on the verge, so I gathered a fulsome bunch of long-stemmed asters, goldenrod, tiny, delicate daisies *(Boltonia),* and added a milkweed pod stalk for good measure.

We drove to the graveyard. The Davis plot was at the top of a steep, pine-tree-clad hill. I thought of the story about the man who gazed down from heaven at his own life. For most of his life's journey the man saw another set of footsteps next to his own: "God, you were there beside me," he acknowledged, gratefully. Then he saw himself progressing through a thorny, lonely stretch. There was only one set of footsteps.

The man turned to God, angry, and cried, "You weren't there! You abandoned me!"

God answered, "I was carrying you."

Today I needed to be carried.

We walked to the top of the hill, where my ex-husband was standing. "Hello, Dith," he said, and we kissed.

Ned had arrived early to dig the hole himself. I went over and looked in. The hole was about two feet square and about four feet deep. The bottom was carefully lined with a bed of tiny boltonia, like a carpet. Later, that daisy carpet, and Ned putting it there, kept coming into my mind. A sandy pile of earth lay next to the hole on a green tarpaulin.

Oh, Neddy! Couldn't we have saved you? God, please oh please roll back the time and bring him back. Please. I'LL DO ANY-THING. Please, oh, please.

I wanted to save you.

"You did this!" you said, in the hospital.

I don't have to torture myself. That won't bring him back.

My mother-in-law and father-in-law's graves were there, and their markers.

The people gathered, walking up the hill. Some of Neddy's aunts and uncles, cousins, a few friends.

It was very hot, and the drone of earthmoving machines came from a sand pit that lay beyond the graveyard. The graveyard itself was a sandpile, too, judging by the sandy earth piled on the green tarp.

Lying next to the hole was a school scarf made of crimson and white wool, the white faded to yellowish with time and the crimson to maroon. The scarf was wrapped around the can of ashes. Or, rather, the can of ashes had been sewn into the scarf, was enclosed in the tube of material. I found out later that Ned had sewn it himself.

One of the priests, Margaret, was standing near the hole and leafing through the prayer book. "Ned and I were just going over the service," Margaret said. "Please join us."

As she once again turned to her book, Ned called to his stepson and left us.

"We were just saying that your nephew Philip will start with this prayer and then I'll say this prayer . . ." Margaret continued. I tuned in and out of what she was saying. I felt a dreadful apprehension, and longed to pace between the gravestones. Others chatted, but I couldn't. I could see Martha tramping back and forth at the further reaches of the graveyard.

"Ned will be holding the ashes and then he will put them in the grave," Margaret's voice came through. I snapped to attention. We looked at each other.

"Oh," she said. "Do you want to hold the ashes, too, and put them in?"

"Of course!" I exclaimed, fiercely. "But if I do," I added, after a minute, "Ned will kill me with his anger."

"No, he won't," she said. "I'll talk to Philip and we'll work it out. We have to have a conference, anyway. After all, Neddy was the child of both of you. And, Dith . . ." she added.

"Why are you calling me Dith?" I snapped. "You can't call me that. It's my family nickname."

She calmly replied, "I'd heard Ned call you that. I didn't know your real name. But now I do, Edith."

"I'm sorry," I said. "I'm terribly anxious." I let out a big whoosh of air and added, "I think you can handle anything I can dish out," I added, grateful that she was a psychotherapist as well as a priest. We had met a few days before for the first time.

"Yes," she said, fixing me with her deep gaze. "Yes. From our visit the other day that's our contract," she said in an intimate and strengthening tone, holding my gaze.

My nephew Philip, who also was a priest, arrived in his white, flowing surplice. Margaret and Philip conferred for a while alone and then called Ned and me over. Soon Margaret said, "Now, in the part of the service where the ashes go into the hole you can either hold them with Edith and put them in with her, or Philip or I will put them in. You can choose what to do."

We waited for Ned to answer. I could see the muscles in his jaw working as he looked down and thought. He seemed agonized. Was I depriving him? Should I rescue him? Give up my wishes? Suppress as of old? There was my "taking care of" instinct again. I kept my mouth clamped shut. Finally he said to Philip, "Why don't you do it." Did he hate me so much he couldn't bear to share this last task for Neddy with me?

Philip turned sternly to me, inquiringly, questioningly. His expression said, Is that O.K. with you?

I hesitated, then said, "Well, I'd really like to put them in together."

"All right. Good," Ned said suddenly. "Why don't we do this.

The ashes are sewn into that scarf that Neddy loved so much. Why don't we take hold of the scarf together and lower it in."

"Fine," I answered, and it was arranged.

"Well, it's twelve o'clock," said Margaret.

Philip and Margaret stood at the edge of the hole.

All of us gathered around. Phil stood on my right, Martha on my left, Ned at her left, and then Elizabeth and the others.

I thought my knees might collapse in the beginning but I gained strength as we went along.

I cried when Philip started his personal remarks. Martha cried throughout.

Philip led off first. He was very upset, very vulnerable, close to tears:

"Cousins. You may not see them all that often, but you just *count* on them being there. I expected to travel through life with Neddy for a long time . . .

". . . He is in God's hands now. The goodness of life has taken him up, ever so gently, knowing that we cannot touch him now. Each one of us will someday turn ourselves over to the good heart that lies behind and within the world itself.

"God bless you, Neddy. God bless you, Ned, and dearest Martha, and dear Aunty Edith. God bless us all."

Margaret said, "In the Christian tradition we acknowledge the tremendous finality of death. The body dies. We return to the earth. Dead is dead. . . . But our tradition also proclaims that in a profound sense, although there has been change, nothing is changed. We are still in the spirit of God—where we began. It is in our belief of God's love that we know hope."

Martha read "Dirge Without Music" by Edna St. Vincent Millay, which ended,

> . . . *Down, down, down into the darkness of the grave*
> *Gently they go, the beautiful, the tender, the kind;*
> *Quietly they go, the intelligent, the witty, the brave.*
> *I know. But I do not approve. And I am not resigned.*

I talked about seeing the whale, and how it made me go back to Neddy's letter and really pay attention. I read the letter out loud and even told them about the joke he had written on the envelope.

His aunt Abigail read a letter she had written:

Dear Neddy,

You are dead. Maybe you don't know that or do you. If you have a consciousness you would know how I feel, but since I doubt this awareness, here goes:

I have a headache, my eyes are flooded and I have no appetite. I am lonely and want to be alone. To say thank you for being you may sound corny but there were many ways I was touched and blessed by you.

First, I think of your energy, playfulness, laughter, anger, rage and smiles. You almost always made me feel special and when you were little we shared secrets. There were many, many times when being with you made a big difference for that day.

Now there is a lump in my throat and a sadness you wouldn't believe but my pain is small compared to all you did and were. We separated some as we aged. That was O.K. Today we are very separate yet maybe I am as close by as I ever was. Listen, you were wonderful.

With much love from your devoted aunt, Gaily.

Phil talked about our mother and the fact that today was her birthday. In my pocket I carried a picture of my mother and me. Then he read a poem called "Pied Beauty" by Gerard Manley Hopkins.

Margaret said, "Spirit of God, we beseech thee to hear the prayers of our hearts.

"We lift up to you our memories of your child, Neddy: our son, brother, lover, friend.

"We celebrate his life. We mourn his death.

"We give you thanks for the sense of wholeness and completion which he experienced in his short lifetime.

"We have been inspired by the courage and persistence with which he overcame obstacles. We have been challenged by his humanness and have been moved by his devotion. We thank you for his groundedness—for his connection to this earth, his body, the world. We thank you for the love he knew which allowed him to love.

"We ask your blessing on us. Neddy's death has angered us, confused us, hurt us. Give us healing and perspective and the knowledge of your love.

"In Jesus' name we pray. Amen."

Philip added:

"In sure and certain hope of the resurrection to eternal life through our Lord Jesus Christ, we commend to Almighty God our brother Neddy; and we commit his body to the ground; earth to earth, ashes to ashes, dust to dust. The Lord bless him and keep him, the Lord make his face to shine upon him and be gracious unto him, the Lord lift up his countenance upon him and give him peace. Amen."

I remember standing at the hole with Ned, holding the long tube of wool, the canister *heavy* at its bottom end, while Ned grasped it above where I did, and lowering it into the grave. Then (Oh, the hardest thing) letting go of the scarf and watching it fall in.

I leaned down and picked up a handful of the sandy earth—some caught under my fingernails—and let it trickle from my hand into the hole. *Oh, no, please don't let it be true.* Numb numbness as I stood there watching everyone else in turn take a handful of dirt and put it in. Martha was crying. I touched her arm. We all stepped back to our former places.

Ned and Martha went again to the grave and dropped some things in. I don't know what Ned put in, but Martha tossed in a letter and two cuff links with the word ACHIEVEMENT on them, and a little red car that was like Neddy's Hot Wheels cars and like his red Toyota, and then I dropped in the Super Ball, and Gaily added her letter.

Then Ned took up the shovel and thrust its blade into the pile and *Oh, that first shovelful—how could he?* tossed the earth into the hole. He worked hard, turning red, to fill the hole, and lifted and heaved and finally peeled up the tarp with its diminished load and poured the last of the dirt on and tamped it down with the shovel. We all went over and helped to put squares of sod and grass on top and make them fit together like a patchwork quilt to keep him warm.

Philip led us in the Lord's Prayer. Then he intoned, "Watch over thy child, O Lord, as his days increase; bless and guide him wherever he may be. Strengthen him when he stands; comfort him when discouraged or sorrowful; raise him up if he fall; and in his heart may thy peace which passeth understanding abide all the days of his life; through Jesus Christ our Lord. Amen.

"O God of peace, who hast taught us that in returning and rest we shall be saved, in quietness and in confidence shall be our strength: by the might of thy Spirit lift us, we pray thee, to thy presence, where we may be still and know that thou art God; through Jesus Christ our Lord. Amen.

"O Lord, support us all the day long, until the shadows lengthen, and the evening comes, and the busy world is hushed, and the fever of life is over, and our work is done. Then in thy mercy grant us a safe lodging, and a holy rest, and peace at the last. Amen."

Margaret read her closing prayer: "Eternal God, you have shared with us the life of Edward Shippen Davis, Jr. Before Neddy was ours, Neddy is yours. For all that Neddy has given us to make us what we are, for that of Neddy which lives and grows in each of us, and for Neddy's life that in your love will never end, we give you thanks.

"And now we offer him back into your arms."

Then it was over.

People walked and talked.

"Hi, honey," Gaily said.

"You're a courageous woman," Margaret said. "I have a completely new perspective."

"I hope you get some peace," Barbara said.

Ned and I didn't speak again, didn't even say goodbye.

Martha and I hung back until we were alone with the grave. *Was that stupid graveyard superintendent still there?* He lounged around all day, a witness. I wanted to shout and scream at him, "Leave us alone!" He leaned against a fence and watched, or watched from his car, and watched and watched and watched, but now I wasn't aware of him.

We sat on the ground, Martha cross-legged.

I put my hand on the quilt and cried.

Where have you gone, Neddy?

CHAPTER SEVEN

The summer was over and I had moved back to my home in New York. One morning, as I sat on the bed, Martha plopped a pile of Neddy's clothes next to me. I gathered it in my arms and sat staring absently at the TV. In the pile were a white knit sports shirt, a brown and white striped Brooks Brothers shirt, a green, white, and blue Drew University shirt, a blue and yellow Gap sweater with diamond motif, his brown corduroy jacket, and his black and red Puma windbreaker.

Soon after Neddy's death, I had gone to his apartment in New Jersey. His clock was still ticking, the sheets were still on his bed, his handwritten note to himself about recycling was taped inside the kitchen cabinet, his razor was on the sink in the bathroom. I took some things I wanted to keep, and I didn't go back. When Martha, her father, and Elizabeth offered to clean out the apartment, I didn't object.

I smelled the clothes, trying to capture Neddy's essence, and encountered a disappointingly impersonal stale smell. Then I found some short, blondish hairs on the inside of the Puma windbreaker. *Oh, God. Hairs from his head.* The clothes were so familiar, and brought him so close, yet he was still so heartbreakingly separate.

Later, I opened the freezer, and there was Bill's ice milk, all ready for him to eat. My rage, which had gone underground for a while, erupted again. Furiously, I melted the ice milk with hot water in the sink, then cleaned out all the cholesterol-free sausages and frozen waffles that we used to have for Sunday breakfast. I snatched Bill's calendar from the refrigerator door, and read the notations in his handwriting about our trip to Woodstock, his son's confirmation, dentist appointments, car insurance payments, and his final day of teaching, before I dumped it in the trash can. I yanked his newspaper clipping on how to tie a bow tie off the corkboard behind the door in the bedroom and threw it away, gathered up from tabletops and bureau drawers and stowed out of sight in my desk the little drawings of us depicted as eccentric rabbits dressed in human clothes and our life together that he had constantly sketched for me. When I had gone away on trips, the clothes in my suitcase had crackled with hidden drawings stuffed in sleeves and stockings. They continued to surface all over the apartment for years.

While I was trying to make Bill disappear, Neddy began to surface more and more. I timed my ride on my stationary bicycle with his stopwatch. I sliced bread on a paddlelike cutting board he'd made. When I took my toast out of the toaster, I used wooden tweezers he had given me so I wouldn't burn my fingers. A pad of writing paper with his name imprinted on it surfaced on my desk.

I was reading a letter from Neddy, and I remarked to Martha, "You know I've saved just as much of your stuff, don't you?"

She exclaimed, "More! Because I've been alive longer."

Martha gave me a book and a card for my fifty-third birthday. On the card she had written, "I hope this book makes you laugh . . . You are very resourceful, strong, loving, understanding, courageous, etc., etc., etc., and I'm proud to be your daughter. I love you, Martha."

She also gave me a box and another card:

"Though I know you have thousands of wonderful pictures you took of Neddy through the 27 very full years of his life, I want to give you the ones I took of him—not many—particularly since I moved to San Francisco.

"I'm sorry this birthday is shot through with losses for you. Please always know and remember that I love you very, very much, and that Neddy did as well. Martha."

I cried when I read that.

"I cried when I wrote it," Martha said.

In the box was a blue leather album containing pictures of Neddy in Ireland, Neddy and the Golden Gate Bridge, Neddy wearing his Gap sweater with the diamond pattern as he recuperated from his heart operation with Martha in Pennsylvania.

On the first page were some quotes in Martha's handwriting:

Death is only a horizon;
and a horizon is
nothing save the
limit of our sight.

—ROSSITER WORTHINGTON RAYMOND

Dying is a wild night
and a new road.

—EMILY DICKINSON

A birthday present from Bill arrived. It was a silver box with a filigreed cover. The message read: "Dear Edith, Please celebrate your nice birthday. All I can say is I'm sorry it didn't work out. You are a dear person to me. Love, Bill."

Martha was packing. She put a big sheaf of paper-clipped papers into her duffel bag. "What are those?" I asked.

"Neddy's research about companies and copies of his applications for jobs. I found them in his apartment."

"What are you going to do with them?"

"I'm not going to do anything with them, just keep them."

His winter gloves, his frying pan, his sweater; she was taking them, too.

She wrote a poem before she left.

The Planets Leave Their Orbits

Now I'm an only child, I thought
the night my brother died.
That, and I miss you
as though the words themselves repeating in my head
could ease me . . . anesthetized
into this brutal undreamed trajectory of my life,
as though missing him as fiercely as I did
might bring him back to comfort me.
Returning to my parents'
homes, I kept waiting for him
to walk through the door, late
and unapologetic in the crush of hugs.
Even at his funeral reception
welcoming cousins left behind years ago
I looked for him among us
wearing his best Brooks Brothers suit
a small smile curling the corners of his mouth
as he inclined his head to listen.
I stood bravely in my black silk dress
holding his absence within me
like a blown-up balloon
burst into tatters.

Last night I dreamt the planets left their orbits,
shooting out beyond the reaches of space
into black oblivion,
the whole order of things disrupted.
On our orphan planet Earth, we wondered
how we would survive
with no natural light or warmth,
how our lives could continue without
our brother planets
orbiting nearby
as they had since galaxies were born.

After Martha had gone, I talked to The Compassionate Friends group leader on the phone. He said, "Oh. Four months. It's so early. At four months I couldn't articulate that I craved, longed for my son's touch. I still have that longing, of course, but I can articulate it now."

I went out to do errands. A whole community of neighborhood tradespeople were helping me through. Naturally, I had told all of them of the tragedy; I even told strangers. The woman at the dry cleaner's welcomed me back after the summer and questioned me closely, intently, to find out how I was; the morose pharmacist at the drugstore who had notarized some of the papers concerning Neddy's estate spoke to me with a tenderness in his voice that hadn't been there in the twenty years I'd known him; the salesman at the eyeglasses store who tightened the screws on my reading glasses was shocked, very shocked. When I got back to my apartment building, the elevator man took me up to my floor. ("No solace. No solace. Only time. Only time," he had muttered, over and over, when he first heard the news.) Now he told me he had lost a daughter ten years before.

One day, rooting around in the kitchen, I came across the pitcher I had used for making baby formula, with tweezers for taking the sterilized baby bottles out of boiling water still stuck in its wide neck. Inside it were black baby-bottle caps and a nipple that I stored there twenty-seven years ago. Time was so strange, and so was my housekeeping!

Martha was safely back in San Francisco and had returned to her job as an editor at a small press and as a massage practitioner. She said on the phone that she had dreamed about Neddy. In her dream, the three of us, reunited as the team we had been since my divorce many years before, were in my apartment. Neddy was curled up, sleeping. Martha knew he would never wake up, but at least he was there, warm, alive. She stroked his hair and he muttered that he loved me.

"Someone gave me a pamphlet that says dreams are real encounters with the dead," I remarked.

"Well, then, maybe he really was speaking to you," Martha answered.

I had decided to visit Pomfret School, the coed boarding school in northern Connecticut that Neddy had attended for three years, from the ages of sixteen to nineteen years old. (Problems caused by dyslexia slowed his education.) Eleven relatives, including his father, uncle, and grandfather, had also attended the school.

A few of my friends couldn't imagine why I wanted to go; it was like rubbing salt into the wound. I knew I had to make the trip, painful as it might be. Throughout the long year of mourning somehow I sensed the right ways to go. They weren't always the easiest ways.

Before I left on the trip, I read letters from Neddy from Pomfret and old diaries about that time in his life.

I had forgotten that Neddy's heart problem was discovered the summer before he started Pomfret. The pediatrician who had treated him since birth had recently retired, and Neddy visited my internist for a routine checkup before starting school. Through his stethoscope, the doctor heard an ominous hissing.

An echocardiogram confirmed a leaky aortic valve. Immediately we visited a cardiologist, who said that Neddy could play sports at school, and that he was in no immediate danger, but emphasized that it was a serious condition.

Neddy adored Pomfret from the first moment that he and I arrived on the campus in the middle of a hurricane. The electricity was out, trees were down, and we found our way through fallen branches to the headmaster's roomy kitchen, where Neddy began to form one of the most important connections of his school career, with the headmaster, the headmaster's wife, and their three sons.

Neddy's first letter home indicated how desperately afraid of drugs and alcohol he was; partly because of his experience with me when I was actively alcoholic, partly because he knew the genetic odds were high that he might develop a drinking problem of his own. He was very disapproving of students who smoked pot or drank and threatened to snitch on them. I don't know if he ever did.

At Pomfret Neddy made the transition from his childhood nickname, Neddy, to his adult one, but, because the latter was identical with his father's nickname, family members continued to call him Neddy. When he came home for his first vacation from school, he said, "To you I'm Neddy, not Ned. Maybe in front of other people you can call me Ned, but at home I'm always Neddy, and you're always Mummy. Maybe in front of other people I'll call you Mom sometimes, but you're really Mummy."

Neddy was under tremendous academic pressure because of the limitations of dyslexia. In the winter of his first year at Pomfret, he was caught cheating on a French test. This resulted in his getting a zero on the exam and being put on academic probation. The expert in dyslexia that Neddy had been seeing for years was called in. She requested that the school eliminate its foreign language requirement in Neddy's case, but the school authorities insisted he finish out the year, even though he was clearly unable to learn the grammar.

During spring vacation I took Neddy to another cardiologist. I had taken both Martha and Neddy to most doctors throughout their childhoods. Since the divorce, I had continued to do so. My ex-husband paid the bills and we conferred regularly on our children's health. This doctor told Neddy outright that he might have to have a heart operation. In the meantime, he could go to soccer camp and play varsity sports. After the appointment, Neddy went around saying, "I may as well drink and smoke pot to make the time go faster. I'm going to die anyway, so why not self-destruct? This is the worst time of my life," until his father and I got him back to his old psychotherapist who had helped him cope with dyslexia.

Perhaps it was at this point that Neddy and I began a pattern that was to grow ingrained over the next eleven years, until the end of his life. That is, since I accompanied him to the doctors until he was old enough to go on his own, I knew the most about his condition and wouldn't let him forget it, even when he wanted to. I was the messenger, carrying a message he often didn't want to hear. I warned against denial.

For instance, when I visited Neddy at summer school in Rhode Island after his first year at Pomfret, I notified the authorities that he had a heart murmur and could only scuba dive down to sixty feet—I'd gotten that figure from his doctor. When he heard that I'd "informed on him," Neddy was furious. He wanted so much to be like the other students. Another summer he attended soccer camp, where he trained and ran hard each day in sweltering August heat. I called his doctor to find out if I should alert the camp directors about his condition. The doctor, who seemed more sanguine about Neddy's condition than I was, finally informed them himself.

The messages I got from the doctors were confusing. They were, "This is a very serious condition. Worry about it. On the other hand, don't worry about it."

In retrospect, I believe that the doctors were caught on the horns of a dilemma: because of the increase in malpractice lawsuits, they were perhaps more cautious about a condition that previously they might have downplayed until a later stage. From my point of view, they were vague or reluctant to inform school authorities about Neddy's condition. I developed the feeling, warranted or not, that I had to pump them for information, and that it was up to me to pass it on to schools, camps, etc. I began to feel, albeit reluctantly, as if I held his life in my hands. Along with this feeling and my need not to leave everything in the doctors' hands, I also held them in awe, as I did to some extent all authority figures.

But we had to live with this, and Neddy's life was full of normal details of teenage development. He had found a girlfriend, he was working hard, he loved Pomfret, he was playing sports.

Sports were always a crucible for Neddy. Despite his relatively small size, he was a fierce competitor. On Parent's Weekend, I had a long talk with Marnie, the wife of the headmaster. She said that Neddy and her son William, who had become inseparable friends, had had a falling out because William got on the varsity soccer team almost without trying and played every game, while Neddy made the team after much difficulty and sometimes sat on the bench for entire games. Neddy began giving William the cold shoulder. Then he began to ignore Marnie, too. Finally she blew up at him, bringing the crisis to a head, and the tension dissipated. While I was visiting, Neddy made a goal in the soccer game, and William was the first to race over to congratulate him.

The theater production that weekend was *Black Comedy* by Peter Shaffer. William was the star. Neddy and I went to see the play together, and I could see why Neddy was jealous of William—he did everything well and with ease, and he was very handsome. Also I thought to myself that William was a good deal more mature than Neddy; certainly, Neddy couldn't have handled a love scene onstage.

Mr. Merjian, a dynamic Armenian who taught English and coached the wrestling team, had brought tears to my eyes in talking about Neddy during my visit that first year. He told me that Neddy's performance on the varsity wrestling team was the most courageous thing he had ever seen. Neddy had lost every match even though he wrestled his hardest. Merj couldn't figure out why Neddy had lost every match. I told him about the dyslexia and a "lazy eye" syndrome. We speculated about whether lack of hand-eye coordination could have accounted for the wrestling losses. Merj said Neddy's gutsiness in sports carried over into his feisty performance in the classroom, where he challenged, questioned, disagreed, probed.

Neddy continued to see doctors. The second cardiologist confirmed the first's diagnosis of congenital valvular disease of the aortic valve. He explained that Neddy's aortic valve was deformed. It had only two lobes instead of three, so blood leaked out each time it beat. It was straining itself by pumping harder than normally to compensate for the leak. The cardiologist said there was no need for surgery at the moment. Right now the heart was getting stronger, as any muscle does when it is strenuously used. In a few years, however, it would start to enlarge. Were it not repaired, it could become weak. The time to operate was on the cusp between enlarging and getting weak.

Neddy spent the two-hour appointment in tears. The doctor warned him that he was handling his condition "by denial," which could be harmful in the long run—that it was much better to acknowledge that he had the condition rather than to act as if nothing were wrong.

Next Neddy had an important test at a hospital. He was so scared and so reluctant to be there that he wouldn't raise his head when the technician was taking his history. He had to swallow a radioactive pill and was hooked up to a machine by electrodes and by a needle in his arm, and then he rode a bicycle while hugging a huge, metal cannonlike camera. The results, cross sections of his heart, emerged in color on a computer terminal. Apparently the test confirmed what the doctor suspected—that his 'regurg' wasn't normal.

All of this put a lot of stress on a student who was already struggling in other ways. Neddy developed a characteristic way of coping. He wrote me from school.

". . . It's been hard but I'll get through it just like I get through all my other pressure systems—[by] hard work."

Pressure systems bring tension. Neddy could exhibit a nasty temper, particularly when he or someone else didn't measure up to his high standards or didn't do what he wanted them to. At one point, he got kicked off the soccer team because he swore at the coach "under" his breath.

Neddy and his girlfriend broke up before the end of his first year, partly because his priority was work, and the girl, a day student, wasn't at school when he was free. Also, Marnie later told me, Neddy didn't feel ready to sleep with the girlfriend, who was a good deal more experienced than he was. Neddy had strong convictions and stood by them. I admired the way he had learned to communicate his feelings and not run away.

In his second year, Neddy and William were back on good terms since they were not competing in a sport, and Neddy resumed visiting the headmaster's family every night after study hall. Marnie said to Neddy, "Take advantage of seeing a happy marriage work—and learn from it. Some people never see it." That gave me a twinge and made me feel sad, but I was happy that Neddy sought them out. It helped also that their youngest son had had open-heart surgery and was an active and normal child. And William was a support to Neddy when he worried about the operation. One day William asked Neddy if he ever prayed. Neddy answered no.

"Then I'll give you a fan."

"Huh? What d'you mean?" Neddy asked.

"You know. A fan. So you can fan yourself in Hell, where you'll go if you don't pray!"

William's threat worked. Neddy prayed.

They had a lot of fun together. That summer Neddy came back from visiting William in New Hampshire and reported that he and William thought Diana, who had become Prince Charles's wife that week, was really good-looking, and that she had probably gotten "royally screwed." Those were horny days; I called Martha at boarding school and she said, "Oh, we're just sitting around reading *The Joy of Sex.*"

In his junior year, Neddy was chosen to be a dorm assistant, a position of honor. Marge and Rich were the faculty couple with young sons who lived in the dorm with the students, and Neddy adored them. In the years after graduation, Neddy often traveled up to Pomfret to stay with them, and they treated him like a third son. He and Rich baked chocolate chip cookies together, and laughed hysterically at each other's jokes. Neddy also made friends with another student, Luis, who was a D.A., too. After the funeral, Luis sat with me in my apartment, holding my hand. "I don't understand," he said. "Ned was always so strong."

In the summer before his senior year I drove Neddy 1,200 miles through Ohio and Pennsylvania to look at colleges. We had a near accident with a dog who ran out on the highway, visited a lovely old town called Marietta on the Ohio River, traveled through Amish country, and took a spur-of-the-moment ride in a helicopter over Gettysburg. Neddy was in fine fettle, pulling down the sunflap in the car to check himself out in its little mirror, exclaiming, "Ah, what a handsome devil!" He prepared for the interviews very carefully, wore a jacket—his green summer jacket that I had bought at Saks—and tie for each one, read each catalog. His six areas of interest were education, psychology, forestry, architecture, theater, and veterinary medicine.

Later that summer Martha and Neddy and I traveled to Ireland for ten days. One of my clearest memories is of Neddy roaring with laughter when I kept turning on the windshield wipers instead of the directional blinker in the unfamiliar rental car. On the Ring of Kerry, he sat on a stoop in front of a yellow door patting a huge brown and white St. Bernard. The dog sat next to him, closing her eyes in ecstasy as Neddy rubbed her head, pulled her ears, and pounded her hard, raising dust from her thick fur, finally embracing her giant head, rubbing his own face on the big face. Later, near ancient beehive huts on a windswept seaside hill, he climbed over a fence into a field and walked down the steep incline to pat a horse. Then he approached a black and white cow, who stared at him warily, rolled her head, showing the whites of her eyes, and backed away.

Neddy visited, with me or his father, more colleges than anyone else in his class and applied to two that were just right for him: Beloit and MacAllister. They were good, somewhat conservative, small colleges in the Midwest, and were probably not as drug involved as other places at the time.

By his senior year, Neddy had become less judgmental of people who might be breaking rules. He hung out less with adults and relied more on his peers. He was very involved with his schoolwork, and had even gotten on the honor roll. His conversation and his vocabulary were increasingly sophisticated. He read the newspaper and had opinions on world events.

Neddy gave me a card with some flowers on Parent's Weekend.

"Here is a small present to you for all your care and love. My grades are O.K. BUT they will go up."

Neddy chose the last three lines of Robert Frost's poem "The Road Not Taken" for his yearbook quote:

Two roads diverged in a wood, and I—
I took the one less traveled by,
And that has made all the difference.

In the spring of senior year, Neddy started freezing me out, rejecting me, separating, which I remember doing with my parents. Really they were too too boring; I was moving on to better things. It hurt terribly to have Neddy turn on me this way, but eventually his sweetness reemerged. One night on the phone he told me, "Whenever we talk about incredible people, I talk about you." He was especially proud that I was sober. One time when he drove home from school with a friend and the friend's parents, he delightedly divulged the news that I was alcoholic. When I protested later that the information was privileged and not meant for casual conversation, Neddy crowed, "If I were you, I'd shout it from the rooftops!"

Neddy had a serious girlfriend now. He had fallen in love with Johanna, another day student at school.

"I've been really happy," he told me soon after the romance started, "and it's only been two weeks."

At graduation, Neddy wore his father's old blue wool Pomfret jacket with its school shield, and white pants. Ned and Neddy and Martha and I tensely posed together for a photo. We attended a chapel service, then filed with the rest of the families into the gym for the graduation ceremony. At lunch I gave Neddy an antique gold coin to add to his coin collection. He had made it through Pomfret, triumphantly.

Pale, watery October sunlight shone on autumn foliage as I drove through Connecticut, finally reaching the towns near Pomfret: Brooklyn, Danielson, Moosup. The tears started when I turned off the highway.

Entering the town of Pomfret, I saw the familiar campus, the red brick school buildings covered with ivy, the stately trees. I parked on the curved driveway in front of the Schoolhouse. Boys and girls carrying books walked to class. A golden retriever nosed in the leaves near the flagpole. Traffic on the main road swished busily by. The soccer field, Neddy's favorite place, was deserted.

It's all still here. There's the headmaster's house. But so what? I feel exhausted. Shall I walk around? Go to the library? Visit the chapel? What a fool I am to look for him here. It's just a place, another place where he isn't.

I decided to visit the white clapboard house in which the admissions office was located. There I encountered Toby, the admissions director, who was just getting off the phone. He shook my hand vigorously and motioned me to a seat in his office. He obviously didn't know what to say. "Words can't . . ." he started out, stiffly, awkwardly. "Dreadfully sorry. Words can't . . ."

I said, "Neddy loved it here. I wanted to come."

"Of course," Toby said, warming up. "May I do anything for you? Call someone on the faculty?"

"No, thanks. I think I'll go to my motel now. I feel tired. Emotion is running high." I was falling back into the old WASPy way of speaking.

"I kind of know what you mean. I hope you'll use us as a base of operations."

"Thank you."

Later I learned that Toby's little girl was diagnosed with diabetes the week before and was hospitalized, so it was especially hard for him to talk to me. Sometimes I could see parents becoming scared of me, as if the death of a child could be catching.

Marge and I went out for dinner. Rich had the flu and couldn't join us. Marge couldn't believe she'd never see Neddy again, expected to run into him around the next corner. She told me she was in Vancouver, British Columbia, with Rich and the children, when she heard the news. It was the first day of Rich's sabbatical. The phone rang, and Ned was on the other end. He told her Neddy had died the night before. It was a horrible, horrible shock. She said she didn't want to come home after the sabbatical, because coming home would make it real.

"We saw him about a month before he died," she told me. "We were staying in New York, and he came in from New Jersey to see us in our hotel. We ordered pizza and watched a baseball game on TV."

"Did he look thin to you?" I asked.

"Yes, but not terribly. Not as if he were going to die. He said he was planning to go to the doctor. He was a little worried."

After dinner, I saw her sons, Peter and David, whom Neddy adored. David wore the DAVID'S COOKIES T-shirt that Neddy had given him six months earlier.

The next day, I had a long talk with Merj. He was a fierce, proud, individualistic man who felt restrained by the boarding-school milieu. He survived by writing a daybook, which he had done for nineteen years, by composing poetry, and by translating American poems for a Soviet newspaper. He had huge, hairy, hamlike arms, and he loved Neddy. He said Neddy fought his way out of the pack and demanded his attention.

"He used to come down to my house and plant trees. Remember? He wanted to be a forester."

"Yes! And he wanted to be a stage manager."

"And he wanted to go into radio! And he would have been a *wonderful* teacher! I didn't see him in banking," Merj added.

"No. Maybe *that's* why his hair thinned so much."

"We were shocked the last time he was here. We thought he might be taking chemo," Merj said.

We talked for an hour. Merj described a warm, loving boy who laughed a lot. Merj's son, Armen, and Neddy were friends. When it turned out that Neddy couldn't win in wrestling no matter how hard he tried, he supported Armen in every match.

Merj gave me a copy of the college evaluation he'd written for Neddy.

I can think of no student I have taught in my twenty-one years at Pomfret who better deserves the title, 'a fighter.' Ned has fought when the odds, certainly the personal odds, were against him.

. . . the adjustment to Pomfret, especially academically, has been tough, and Ned has had to face great frustration in the class-room and on the playing field. His integrity, fortitude, and self-discipline in the face of disappointment has been a model for all of his classmates; his attainment of excellence and honors in academics and varsity soccer, however, have been triumphs. . . . I think of Ned as a tough bulldog who stands guard over the portals of his own future: tenacious, full of heart, willing.

. . . Over the past two years I have, sorting out the many hours of talk between us, been able to point to one of Ned's strengths which separates him from others his age—his honesty in assessing his own strengths and weaknesses, his pure-of-heart goodness, his lack of malice, and most of all, his sense of the individual to overcome. This sense of overcoming is precocious, for it encompasses the need for enduring some hardships, some personal pain, and some sacrifices. This from a kid who has had everything, yet wants to make a life for himself which is not silver-lined and elitist, removed from the real concerns of the world.

. . . I enthusiastically endorse Ned's personal, academic, social and intellectual qualifications for higher education. This 'fighter' is a person much to be sought.

After I left Merj, Marge and I walked over to the soccer field to look at the star magnolia tree that she and Rich had donated to the school in Neddy's memory. The grounds crew had just planted it on a little rise, facing the goal, and were tamping down the dirt. It was a sturdy, bushy shrub, and would bloom in the spring.

There were a few players on the field, kicking the ball and

taking headers. We watched for a while. Marge murmured, "Sometimes you can almost see him out there." And you almost could: his blond hair shining, his face flushed from running, his legs strong, taking the penalty kick, first knocking his cleated shoe against his other high-socked leg to get the mud off.

"Sometimes you can almost see him out there."

After lunch, I wandered outside. It was seventy degrees and beautiful. At the deserted football field, sitting on a bench and holding my sides, I sobbed.

A week later, I had lunch with Marnie in New York.

She told me that William had driven all the way up from Virginia for the funeral. I hadn't really thanked him for coming, because I was crying too hard to talk when he reached me in the huge receiving line in the church. I told Marnie to tell him how much I appreciated his coming to the funeral. She said William and his wife were expecting a baby the next week. That was so wonderful and yet the news went through me like a knife.

Marnie gave me two books by bereaved parents. She wrote in one, "For Edith. There are no words except that I am loving you."

Marnie's brother and sister had both died many years before. Her sister was only six and Marnie was two years younger. Her brother had committed suicide twenty-seven years ago when he was a teenager.

Marnie said her intense involvement with the kids at Pomfret arose from her feelings about her brother; that she couldn't bear to see anyone, particularly adolescents, unhappy like her brother was, so she really threw herself into it. I told her how wonderful she was to the kids at school and how very important she was to Neddy.

"God must love you a lot," she said, "because He's testing you. He ordained all this. Even if you'd taken Neddy by the scruff of his neck and dragged him to the doctor, it wouldn't have made any difference. It was meant to happen this way."

She described near-death experiences—how people go through a tunnel with a light at the end, how they feel peace beyond all understanding, how they resent being revived.

She spoke about Jesus, holy ghost, and holy spirit, and urged me to find comfort in the church. There was, she said, a kind of reform in the Episcopal Church, and she was very involved. Church to her had been boring and barbaric, before she began to believe. Her faith comforted me.

CHAPTER EIGHT

After Pomfret, the news kept announcing itself to me, over and over, like a dull hammer blow: he's never coming back, *he's never coming back*, HE'S NEVER COMING BACK. It was a double whammy: Neddy and Bill. I felt almost suicidal, and less willing to talk about it.

There was nothing left now but the pain of knowing. I had been so very brave; I was tired of being brave.

In some ways I was acting so normal people would be surprised to learn my real state of mind. Because it was unacceptable to me to feel this despairing, I covered it up.

I talked to my friend who had lost her son and husband. She said, "Wanting to die is part of grieving. At first the pain is dulled by shock. But later, shock wears off. Some people close off from the pain, become bitter, and let it ruin their lives; but there's a way of going into and through it which can bring rebirth."

Another friend pleaded, "Don't despair." I asked myself, what else is this about, anyway, if not despair, and feeling it?

I read a review of a book about a woman who traced the son she had given up for adoption many years before. The arduous and wrenching process of finding him was a testament to the bonding power of motherhood. For a moment, instead of being apologetic, I saw my preoccupation with Neddy, my wish to be near him, my need to review his life, as necessary, natural, a gift, a quest, a holy war, a test in fire, something that was going to save my life.

Nevertheless, I resolved to see my therapist at least once a week.

From Martha:

. . . I agree with you that in some ways it gets harder. It's very hard right now. For me, receiving and having to decide what to do with Neddy's employee stock and particularly his life insurance money is really the pits . . . I really hate that there's money tied up with Neddy's death and I wish I could be more grateful to him. Several people have said how moving it is that he thought of me, took care of me this way. But all I feel is anger and desolation—I don't care about the damn money, and I hate thinking about how thoughtful and caring it was of him. The money will help me, but it's a lousy compensation. There is no compensation. All I want is Neddy back.

One day I had an interview with a reporter who was writing a magazine article about me.

After she left my apartment, I went into the bedroom. The bulb in a lamp had blown out, and I unscrewed it, but I was all out of bulbs to replace it. I looked at the socket and imagined plunging my finger in.

I didn't want to be in the magazine if Neddy couldn't know. How could I accept recognition? How could I act normal or even happy for the pictures they wanted to take?

When the event happened, however, it turned out to be a joyful occasion. The magazine story was to commemorate the anniversary of the publication of *Pat the Bunny,* the biggest-selling American children's book, which had been written and illustrated for me by my mother.

At the photo shoot, I concentrated on how lucky I was to have been the first little baby—there had been over six million of them since then—to enjoy my mother's book. The photographer placed a medium-sized brown rabbit on my shoulder. It sat there, warm and softly breathing, its fur velvety against my cheek, while I gently read the words from the book over and over.

A photograph of the brown rabbit sitting on my shoulder and the story appeared in the magazine about a month later. It looked as if the rabbit was reading the book I was holding. I learned from the experience that I could laugh and have fun without being disrespectful or disloyal to Neddy.

In November, I often walked in Central Park. The trees had lost most of their leaves. The days were shorter, the air crisp. Sometimes I ate lunch in the playground where I used to take the children when they were small. It was pleasant to sit in the sun in a sheltered spot out of the wind.

One day a four-year-old boy started talking to me. He told me he didn't like chicken soup, which I was eating out of a paper cup. Then he got ready to go to the zoo with his father, putting on his little jacket. At first I thought he was going to put it on like Neddy did—laying it down on the ground upside down and then putting his arms in the armholes and whipping it over his head onto his back, but he just put it on backwards, like a hospital johnny robe. I enjoyed the joke with him.

Martha wrote me again:

> . . . I wanted to say, among other things, that I've been appreciating your empathy with how I must be feeling as his sister. That you've been thoughtful and supportive and loving. My friends here, many of them, are going through hard times, and they seem to want to link our feelings, to commiserate, and I often find that alienating. ([But] . . . sometimes hurt is just hurt, and I can feel that connection.) I am also impressed with the ways that you are taking care of yourself and listening to your needs . . .
>
> Well, I need to get going, but this letter has millions and gazillions of particles of love in it, swirling all around you, like a big hug.
>
> Love love love love love love love love love, Martha

I continued to seek out activities that made me feel better. A friend and I took a cooking course, although in less stressed times I really didn't like cooking very much. Now it seemed the most calming, nurturing thing in the world. My lexicon soon consisted of shoyu, adzuki beans, bulgur, kasha, umeboshi plums, millet croquettes, peanut-kuzu cream. Later, as my fervor oozed away, kale and collard greens grew limp in the refrigerator.

An urge to move furniture seized me. I pushed the little sofa from next to the fireplace down to the end of the living room near the windows. This was the only place in the apartment where sun streamed in at certain hours of the day. I placed a butler's table in front of the little sofa, and put a vaseful of pretty flowers on the table. I began to sit there in the morning with my portable phone, or the newspaper, or a book.

I became obsessed with an idea for a painting. I had only done a few finished paintings in my life. The most successful was the one of Neddy with his bike which hung over the fireplace. Now I had the idea of doing a big painting of boats. I could see the design in my mind. The boats were rowboats. They were slightly skewed from the viewer's point of view, and you looked down on their interiors from above.

An artist friend came up to my apartment and stretched a canvas for me. It was large, five feet by four. I primed it with two coats of plain Matte Medium and two coats of Matte Medium mixed with acrylic white. After that, I propped it against the wall in Neddy's old room, where it stayed, untouched, for many months. The mechanics of actually making the painting seemed too exhausting and too difficult to actually carry through.

I still woke in the morning heavy with the knowledge that Neddy was dead. Even though the grief was still incredibly pervasive, and I often felt that my life had stopped, it wasn't really true. I had resumed my normal routine. I saw friends and had lunch or dinner, attended lectures, went to the movies. I ate out in restaurants, and met with publishers and editors about future work.

My children's book career was in low gear. The story about the sea otter had been turned down. A book about colors was due to be published in the spring. A series I was planning was still taking shape in my mind. My most important task at the time was writing my journal. I worked on it every day.

I had vowed to myself to take photographs for a year as a kind of tribute to Neddy, so I forced myself to travel around the city with my camera. I hid it under my coat on the subways because I was afraid of getting ripped off. By the end of the year, I had pictures of a snowstorm on Park Avenue at night, the World Trade

towers in the mist, student cooks in uniforms and chef's hats learning "knife skills" in Chelsea, pool players in a pool hall in Soho, a
violinist serenading passersby near the Bethesda Fountain, a
courtly doorman helping a dowager out of a cab on upper Fifth
Avenue, a sidewalk Santa at the Seaport Museum, shoppers entering a store on the Lower East Side, live carp in a tank in China-
town. Some of the pictures I took that year were later included in
a showing of my photographs at a gallery on Madison Avenue.

My friends were generally supportive and nonjudgmental about
how I was handling the grief, but one old schoolmate drove me
crazy. She called all the time with a jolly, forced jocularity. She
had made me into her "mission." She pronounced that my problem was guilt. "I wish that I could turn the key and release you,"
she stated.

I was very defensive. I said, "Yes, I DO feel guilty, but EVERY-
ONE at The Compassionate Friends does, no matter what the
circumstances, and I'm working through it."

"Well, I *wish* we could just kidnap you and get you out here to
Arizona."

"I'm perfectly happy where I am, thank you."

"I'm coming to New York next week and I definitely want to see
you."

"Well, um, I'm terribly busy."

"Oh, I *know* you are but I just want to catch a glimpse of you."

It was the *control* that was so annoying, or maybe it was the
assumption on her part that I was helpless, and if only she could
take over, everything would be all right. It was infantilizing.

I had lunch with an acquaintance who had always seemed ditsy,
nervous, anxiety-ridden, but when we started talking, she was very
focused; her son had also died.

I told her that I had gone to Pomfret, and some people wondered why I put myself through such an ordeal. "You had to go.
Everyone who loved your son is sacred," she said, fiercely, con-
firmingly.

She believed that the time of our birth and the time of our
death is preordained, "stamped on our ticket."

When I got home, I opened an old diary, and some dried-up old
flowers fell out. They were flowers from my cousin Pammy's coffin,

and they had been in the diary thirty-seven years. It was very important, at the time, to preserve something, to have something to hold.

Every new death brings up echoes of others, and emphasizes the bewildering imponderability of God's plan.

Every day I prayed for God's will for me, and trusted my intuition to lead me to the next right action. At this point I still found it incredibly painful to contemplate the details of Neddy's final illness, but I gradually realized that I had to know exactly what had happened from his internist. With trepidation—I had to walk around the block twice—I went to Dr. K's office and made an appointment to see him.

Jim was standing in the hall as I left the reception area. He looked thinner and older. He was talking to someone but said, "Hello, Edith."

I answered, "Hello, Jim." I waited until he had finished his conversation, and then stated, "I just made an appointment to talk to you on Monday, because I still have some questions about Neddy."

He answered, "Good, Edith."

I said, "I couldn't get up the courage to call you," and began to cry.

He answered, soothingly, "You don't need courage to come here, Edith."

Crying, I muttered, "It *feels* like I do."

He looked into my eyes and affirmed, "It's a terrible loss. A terrible loss."

When I came back a few days later, Jim told me what had happened. He read from Neddy's chart.

He saw Neddy three times in April, two months before Neddy died. The first time he saw him, Jim gave him a shot of penicillin because he had a dental appointment. Neddy had to take antibiotics every time he went to the dentist to ward off infection from bacteria which might be dislodged from his mouth and travel into the bloodstream. Anyone who has an implant, like Neddy's implanted heart valve, is susceptible to such infection and must take antibiotics when undergoing any dental work. Neddy had lost weight so Jim asked him to return soon.

The second time Jim saw him, Neddy was clearly sick. Jim suspected endocarditis, an inflammation or infection of the heart lining or valve. He tested for four criteria: red spots on the body, which Neddy didn't have; elevated sedimentation rate, Neddy's was slightly up but nothing serious; anemia, his white blood count was up but not bad; and red corpuscles in the urine, which Neddy didn't have, either. Neddy was exhausted and had lost fifteen pounds.

The third time that Jim saw him, the white blood count was better, the sed rate was down from forty to twenty-seven, there were no red corpuscles, and no red spots. Still, Jim continued to be concerned. He called Neddy and said, "We haven't figured out why you've lost weight, so you must come back again." That was about six weeks before he died. Neddy made two more appointments but broke both of them, so Jim never saw him again.

I asked, "If he hadn't broken the appointments, would he have survived?"

"Yes," Jim replied. "Because all of the criteria would have been present."

It was the heart attack that killed him. How Jim thought it must have happened—he drew a picture—was that the strep viridans, which lives in the mouth, may have traveled down through the bloodstream and lodged in the pig valve, creating an infection. Probably after that a piece of the infected valve broke off, clogging a pulmonary artery, and then Neddy had a heart attack that involved 20 percent of his heart.

I asked, "Could he have survived the heart attack? Would he have been impaired?"

"Yes, he could have," said Jim. "And yes, he would have been severely limited. Also, he would have had to have another valve replacement operation very soon—which would have been very difficult, if not impossible, because of the heart attack."

I said, "On that last day—if he had gone to the emergency room at the hospital in New Jersey, what would have happened?"

"The result would have been the same. It was too late."

"But he wouldn't have had that terrifying drive from New Jersey to the city," I said.

"Neddy knew Dr. G and trusted him, and Dr. G was in New York . . ."

"He was looking for a doctor in New Jersey," I interrupted, bitterly. Then, "Why didn't you hospitalize him?" I burst out.

"I've talked to people about that," Jim answered, looking upset. "The hospital administrator would have refused to hospitalize him, by law, since he didn't have any symptoms. And, if somehow he *had* been hospitalized, and they didn't find anything, he would have received the whole bill, $15,000. If Neddy was struggling financially before that, a $15,000 hospital bill would have been staggering. Of course, in hindsight, who cares?"

I talked about my guilt—that I was the only one, besides himself, who had been gravely concerned about Neddy's health, so I felt I should have saved him. Jim said sternly, "He was a twenty-seven-year-old man, an intelligent man, not a five-year-old! You can't do that to yourself, Edith."

Then I asked, "Can drinking during pregnancy cause defects, deformations in the heart?"

"No," Jim said, definitively. "Just low birth weight."

"But I've read about it. Drinking can cause eye problems like Martha's and malformations of the heart like Neddy's."

"No," he said. "My wife drank like a fish and smoked when she was pregnant, and our three kids are fine."

"My niece," he added, after a moment, "lives in Minneapolis. Last week she was outside a museum waiting for her husband to come out. She had their month-old baby in a pouch carrier. After half an hour or so of walking up and down, she said to herself, 'Hmmm. The baby hasn't moved in a while.' When she looked, the baby was dead."

Then he told me that a friend's eighteen-year-old daughter had been kidnapped from her dorm and raped, and, trying to escape, was shot and killed. "Her parents are all right, but . . ." he said.

"Yeah, I'm all right, but . . ." I muttered, and sobbed.

"I can't imagine what it feels like, Edith, the depths of your sadness. I don't know if I could bear it if anything happened to my Anna . . ."

"You bear it, Jim, somehow . . ."

I asked him why Dr. G, the cardiologist, kept repeating, "I can't answer your question," over and over in our phone conversation.

Jim was shocked. "Why do you think he did that?" he asked.

I added that Dr. G had refused to meet with me in person.

Jim gasped and rolled his eyes. "Do you want me to get him to see you?"

"No, I don't need to anymore."

After a silence, I asked, "Do you think there would be any point in talking to the nurse who was there when Neddy died?"

"No," Jim answered, "but I could arrange it for you if you want."

"Well, no. I guess not. That's okay."

I thought a moment and then said, "I don't believe you, Jim, about the drinking while I was pregnant."

"Look," he said, leaning forward over his desk, "suppose it could have happened that way, so what? You weren't warned and so what?"

In a little while he added, "My mother always said to me, 'Jim, why do you keep worrying about things that are already over?' When I was a senior in college, I was asked to Bermuda, and I was very disappointed because I had to turn the invitation down. Then, six months later, I was asked again, and I accepted. My mother was sick, but I went to Bermuda.

"Mother died two days later. I rushed home, and I said to my sister, 'I *wish* I'd been here.'

"My sister said, 'Well, Mother was in a coma all day.' But Mother had a black nurse named Hazel.

"Hazel said, 'No, that's not true, Jim, your mother called out for you all day.' Now, I'm such a guilty person that I started to worry, but then I remembered what my mother said: 'Don't worry about it, it's already over.' "

I could tell he still felt guilty, fifty or so years later. But it was sweet of him to tell me the story.

He went on. "I can't tell you not to worry or to feel guilty or sad. I do know it takes a long, long time." He paused. "Thank you for coming in, Edith. I was afraid I'd run into you."

"I couldn't come here before this. I was so *angry.*"

We hugged.

"Please call me any time if you have any more questions."

"May Martha see you if she wants to?" I asked.

"Of course."

Later, irrationally, I wondered why I had been so nice to him, and I blamed him for not knowing how ill Neddy was, even though he didn't seem to have been at fault.

CHAPTER NINE

Thanksgiving started the long, gloomy parade of holidays, culminating with Neddy's birthday in January.

Normally I didn't care so much about Thanksgiving, but it turned out to be sharply painful. The previous year Neddy, Elizabeth, Martha, and Bill's mother had come over for Thanksgiving dinner. There were pretty flowers on the table, turkey, cranberry sauce, turnips and onions, mashed potatoes, ice cream, pumpkin pie. Neddy and Bill washed the dishes.

This year the day passed with agonizing slowness, ending with my giving money to homeless people on the street as I walked home from visiting friends.

I ran into someone I knew, who asked, "How are you?"

"I've had a really rough day."

"Is it the same thing?" he asked.

"Yes! Neddy's dead!"

"I mean, it isn't anything new, is it?"

Martha had last seen Neddy on Thanksgiving weekend a year ago, which they spent with their father at his house on Long Island. They took a long walk through snowy fields and had a snowball fight.

On the drive into the city on Sunday afternoon, Neddy made a racist joke, and Martha strongly objected. He didn't seem to understand her explanation of why what he said was "wrong." Then they wrangled about her buying her car. He couldn't fathom why she needed one when there was such a thing as public transportation in San Francisco. She explained that she used the car to see clients, transport her massage table, and go to work at the publishing company. The fact that she might use it for something fun, like going to the mountains, was too frivolous for Neddy. And the fact that she had used some of her savings to buy the car was beyond him. He was *very* critical and judgmental. They ended up yelling at each other.

Martha and I talked on the phone about how Neddy's hard-driving mentality led to his death.

"I just want to say to him, 'Look where your philosophy got you, jerk!' " Martha said. Then she added, "There was a lot about my life that he didn't get."

I said it was sad he worked in a bank, such a boring job.

Martha remarked that she thought he was happy in his job. She would have been bored stiff working at a bank, but he seemed to like it.

We talked about his psychotherapist and I wondered if she knew that Neddy had died.

Martha said, "He told me she said she thought he was one of the most well-adjusted people she knew—that he was practical and realistic."

I said I didn't think that he was.

"I don't, either," Martha said. "The thing that bothers me most was his low self-esteem. He never thought he was good enough. Getting sick at the end was just another failure." She was near tears.

There was a pause. Finally I said, "I hope he knows how successful he was."

We thought about that.

"I still do bargaining," Martha declared.

"What do you mean?"

"I made three new friends this year, and they've helped me most of all. They mean so much to me. Sometimes I walk around saying, 'I'll give them up if you'll just give him back. Please, please, give him back.' "

"My bereaved sober friend says that she'd drink if it would bring her child back. So would I."

"Yes."

We were silent for a few moments.

"I don't like to think that the last time I saw him I was *screaming* at him. Even though later we talked on the phone and wrote long letters and resolved our argument."

"I yelled at him, too, the last time I spoke to him," I said.

"I know."

Martha asked, "You know what? This is going to sound strange. The clasp of my watch is broken. I mean, it keeps popping open. And it reminds me of him. I mean, it's like he's trying to get in touch. So every time it pops open, I say, 'Hi, Neddy.' "

As Christmas approached, I remembered the old days.

One Christmas Neddy and I had bought our tree on the street about four blocks from my apartment. Evergreens leaned up against ropes strung along the periphery of the sidewalk. A man wearing a puffy down parka and a stocking cap wrested a tree out from the lineup and held it upright so we could assess its shape. "Sixty-five dollar," he said. "Just in from South Carolina."

Neddy and I looked at each other, frowning. "That's too expensive," I declared.

"Besides, a tree should be from the North, not the South," Neddy murmured. "The North Pole, if possible."

"This is a balsa," said the man, wrenching another tree out of the lineup. "It's from Nova Scotia. You can have it for forty-five."

I stepped back and gazed at the tree. It was bushy and its branches were fairly even, but it had a long, naked trunk. "What do you think?" I whispered to Neddy, my breath visible in the frosty air.

"I think the prices here are terrible, just terrible," Neddy answered loudly. "You should see how cheap trees are near school." He was twenty-two years old, and still in college.

"I know. I know. But this is the city. O.K. Yes," I said, turning to the salesman. "Can you trim off the trunk, please?"

"Sure." The man slid the tree into a horizontal barrel-like contraption and pushed until the trunk protruded through the hollow barrel. He cut off five inches with a Swedish saw. Then he dragged the tree through the barrel. When it came out, the tree's branches were squashed up against its trunk and plastic netting enclosed them, making a tidy package for carrying.

Neddy took the heavy end and I hefted the light. We set out for home. We had to rest several times, and Neddy ended up carrying the whole tree.

Later we decorated the tree with faded glass bells from my childhood, taken with care from their year-round resting places in old De Pinna boxes. We added a tin candy cane and two tin angels with arched wings that Martha had made in third grade, sand dollars from a long-ago trip to Bermuda with wire hangers fitted into their natural slots, a glass snowflake, a red papier-mâché pig, icicles, bells with Audubon scenes, and various other ornaments that had been acquired over the years. The tree was topped by a star with uneven points and concentric bands of iridescent colors: green, purple, and a yellow center, which Martha had also made. We never used electric lights on the tree and didn't even own them.

A small frosted bulb illuminated a little house with a slanting roof and open front that stood on a shelf near the fireplace. The crèche was from my childhood home. Every year I took the painted plaster figures out of their crumpled tissue paper and placed them gingerly on the ancient straw that lined the floor of the box. I put the three kings, stately figures with long robes, in the interior of the box. Then I carefully positioned the Christ child in his tiny manger in the site of honor in the center. Mary, Joseph, three shepherds, and two kneeling cows, one with its plaster horns chipped off, exposing two wires, clustered around him.

On Christmas Eve, Neddy and I attended the Christmas pageant at our church. Bill didn't join us, as he was shopping. He did most of his Christmas shopping at the very last moment, enjoying the crowds and the madness.

Neddy and I attended the pageant every year. We loved to watch children from the church school acting out the story of Jesus' birth. Every year Mary, wearing blue and riding on the same patient, redolent donkey, was turned away from the inn by the innkeeper. Every year the Three Kings, followed by tiny attendants holding their robes and who invariably tripped as they climbed the chancel steps, came to worship the newborn Babe. Every year the shepherds, dressed in ruglike skins and carrying crooks, brought live, baaing sheep to join the throng. Every year adolescent girl tumblers did their cartwheels and landed with loud thumps on the floor, and a choir of spotlit winged angels sang "Silent Night" from a balcony high above the congregation. We watched for details and poked each other with satisfaction when they came.

Later, after Martha arrived from California, we laid our stockings on the floor in front of the fireplace; there was no mantel from which to hang them. We omitted the graham crackers and milk for Santa, now that everyone was grown up. When the children were small, we had always left a plate of graham crackers and a glass of milk for Santa as a treat when, hungry and tired, he slipped down the chimney during the night. Santa had usually scrawled a thank-you note in jagged, messy handwriting, drained the glass of milk, and scattered graham-cracker crumbs all around and left big, ashy footprints on the rug.

The next morning, clad in pajamas and bathrobes, we emptied our stockings on Bill's and my big double bed, and then got ready to open presents.

"Hey, wait a minute," Neddy said, rubbing his eyes. "I'm going to put my contacts in." He headed toward his bedroom. Both Martha and Neddy wore contact lenses.

"I'm hungry," said Bill. "I could use a coffee ring with nuts, sugar, and raisins."

"Mmmm. Me, too," said Martha.

"Martha, how was your concert last week?" I asked.

"It was pretty bad," answered Martha, who was looking tired after her late-night arrival. "Our chorus did Bach's *Magnificat* live on the radio, and we messed up the beginning, so we had to start over again. It was very embarrassing."

"Oh, no."

"I've gotten over it now," said Martha.

"I'm ready. Let's go," said Neddy, coming back into the hall where we stood waiting for him. Our old tradition was that we lined up, youngest first, and marched into the living room to see

Christmas revealed. Now Neddy pushed me ahead of him into the living room, saying, "We're all grown up now, remember? Hey, before we open presents, I've got a special one for all of you. It won't take long. I promise. It's really special. You have to sit down."

We took seats facing Neddy, who stood next to the Christmas tree. He held a piece of paper.

"I even typed it."

"This is a toast. I wrote it last night. I even typed it," Neddy announced. He composed himself, stood very straight, and started reading. "First, to my dearest sister. It only seems like last week that we used to play out in the Cowboy House in Brookfield, or play house with those cheap dinnerware plates. Unfortunately, we have grown up. But fortunately, we have not grown apart. Even with you clear on the other side of the United States, I feel that you are really not that far away. You're just a little to the right of my desk, where I keep my pad of paper that I write to you with. Your letters have been very interesting and full of fun, something I tried to return. Anyhow, what I really wanted to say is thank you for being a friend and a great pen pal!! But mostly, I want to thank you for being you. And for your first Christmas present, I want to give you a *big* hug and a kiss."

"Thank you, Neddy," said Martha, jumping up and hugging her brother tightly. "You're a great bro. I love you too."

Martha sat down and Neddy continued to read.

"Secondly, to Bill," he said, quite formally, turning to face Bill, who sat up straight in his chair. Neddy and Bill had become quite close in the year and a half that Bill had been around.

"I think it's a good sign that I can't remember when you first started living here, but as I look back at the last twelve months, I can see that you have added your own particular set of colors to this household. Yes, I believe that you are sort of like a magician; a little humor here, a little art there, and presto! happiness has entered into my mother's life like never before. I hope that I am not putting words in her mouth but I think that she is very grateful that you are around. I too am very grateful that you have been around to add your sense of humor. So, I want to thank you for being a friend of mine and also to my mother. I also want to thank you for talking and listening to me when the subject needed a gentleman's perspective. I want to give you as your first Christmas present a *big* hug and, if you want it, a kiss."

Bill, blinking fast behind his eyeglasses, got up and hugged Neddy and then sat down again. He wiped a tear from his eye.

"Oh, Neddy. How beautiful," I murmured.

"Now for the old Mom," Neddy said, and began to read again. "And last but far from the least, my most precious mother. O.K., so I really blew it sometimes. As a matter of fact, if one is going to count the times, you will need more than eight fingers and two thumbs. But let's not dwell on the less fortunate times, and move on to the exciting ones. I firmly believe that these last twelve months have been a time for your own personal success and for *our* success. I have learned a great deal—like, one day at a time, easy does it, and even how to take naps in the middle of the day. I think that you are the best mother, one hell of an author/editor, and of course all those other things that go into being a great person. So, along with the now standard *big* hug and a kiss, I would like to end this letter with the three words that any mother wants to hear from her son or daughter. I Love You!!!!!!!"

Martha arrived safely from California for the third time since Neddy's death. I had cooked for hours and served up a meal of ginger fish, couscous with combu seaweed stock and a red cabbage and chicory salad with shoyu dressing. It was very good. Martha thought there was hope for me, as a cook, yet.

The next day we bought a tree and carried it home together. We set it up and got the Christmas tree decorations out of the closet. We lit a candle in the living room in Neddy's memory.

Martha had gone to a grief group in California where they suggested writing to the deceased on paper Christmas decorations. She had brought cutouts of flying doves along with her, and we colored and wrote on them.

Martha's read, "Dear Neddy: I want to be merry and joyful this

"Love, Big Sis."

Christmas because you would be if you were here, but I miss you too much. Love, Big Sis."

Mine said:

"Dear Neddy,

Wherever you are—

Merry Christmas!

I love you, Mummy"

And on the other side of the same bird:

"Dear Neddy,

Fly high!

Soar!"

We hung the birds on the tree.

On Christmas Day, Martha and I emptied our stockings, then sat in the living room and opened presents. We expressed our gratitude for being together, for the fire in the fireplace, for friends and family, for living in a country not devastated by war, for having enough food to eat and a roof over our heads.

After dinner, Martha asked me to read her essays for grad school, so I did, and wrote comments, and we spent an hour sitting side by side, shoulders touching, improving the sentences. It was a lovely, quiet, sharing time.

Martha said, "Don't die—ever."

I answered, "Well, don't you, either."

"I'll try not to do it before you."

CHAPTER TEN

To pass from the year Neddy died seemed simply terrible.

Someone said, when I acknowledged I was terrified of leaving the old year behind, of leaving Neddy behind, "Well, why don't you just pack him up and take him with you?"

I thought about it for days and then wrote a poem.

Please Come Too

Pack you up
And take you along,
They said.
How?
How?
You are not the pictures.
You are not the letters or the movies or the video.
You are not the suit in the closet.
Or the voice on the tape.
Or the ashes.

You are not the empty room.
Or the tears of your lover.
Or your sister's moans.
Or your father's pain.

Or my agony.
You are gone.
As gone as a bird
That flies out of sight.
As gone as the grape
On the vine.
As gone as smoke
Rising into the air.
As gone as the taste of food
Upon the tongue.

(Cruel.
Cruel.
What kind
Of God are You?
God damn
You.)

And yet—
What is that
In my heart?
You are there,
My son.
My love for you
Is there.
It can come with me
Into the New Year.

Please come too.
You're already dead
Six months;
This isn't new.
Please come, too.
Please come, too.

On New Year's Eve, the guilt at not saving Neddy came up strongly again, as it always did in times of deeper grief. I read a story in a magazine about a parent who was arrested for ingesting cocaine when she was pregnant. Could I be arrested, charged (tried? executed?) for drinking alcohol, taking aspirin, smoking, drinking coffee, while I was pregnant?

There was an article in the paper about sperm causing defects in fetuses. It said, "Several studies have found that fathers who take two or more alcoholic drinks a day have smaller than average infants" and ". . . certain substances in sperm can lead to permanent defects in children. These include familiar birth defects like heart abnormalities . . . as well as less familiar ones like childhood cancer and learning disorders." There was no reason I had to carry all of the guilt all of the time.

Someone asked me, "Have you been keeping yourself busy?"

"No," was my answer. "I haven't. I've been slowing down so I can feel the feelings. Fending them off really hurts. But I feel so alone. The early grief was like a connection, and now there's only a void. It's almost as if he was never here at all. And yet, I'm terrified of leaving behind the year in which he was alive. I'm still so angry at God."

My friend who had lost her son and husband called. She said, "I don't believe that God caused our tragedies. I believe that the universe is cruel, and that God is the healing."

I told her about someone who had implied that I was impeding Neddy by staying stuck in the grief. My friend commented that she didn't believe that we could impede the dead, but, "we would if we could." She added that they are "not in time—not our time, anyway."

At a few minutes to midnight, I sat in the living room. I wore Neddy's Drew cap (the sweatband stained by his sweat).

Now is the last time I can say, "My son died this year."

God, he's passing farther and farther away. Can't you send me a sign? That he's O.K.? Please?

Time, which had been abnormally attenuated since June 20, 1990, speeded up after January 1, 1991, rushing toward Neddy's birthday.

Soon after the new year started, I received a letter from my ex-husband. Well, it wasn't a personal letter, it was a copy of his letter to the lawyer in New Jersey who had settled Neddy's estate. The letter was a complete accounting of Neddy's estate when he died. This money was going to Martha. How sad, how very sad the figures seemed. Ned had been dealing with cruelties. I was touched he sent the numbers to me.

I came across a strange news item. Scientists wanted to test a strand of Abraham Lincoln's hair to obtain medical information on whether he had a disease called Marfan syndrome. *Oh, God. Can't you duplicate a person by cloning? What if Neddy could be cloned from his hair that I kept from his first haircut? Wouldn't that be obscene? Would he have to live an exactly identical life? And go to his early death?*

A new little Neddy, at the age of his first haircut, all ready to grow up again, and be . . . different? The same?

I had a good therapy session with Kathy. She thought it was progress that my feelings were simply, "I want to die because I'll never see him again," instead of, "I should be punished because I made him die and I'll never see him again." I agreed. It was clear to both of us that, although I wanted to be dead—escape—I did not really want to kill myself.

I told Kathy about the several letters of sympathy, which Martha showed me, to my ex-husband that said, "You are the person Neddy loved best in the world," and that the wall in Neddy's apartment was covered with pictures of him and his father.

"He wanted his approval?" Kathy asked.

"Yes."

"He already had yours?"

"Yes."

"Children relate completely differently to a mother and a father. It's not comparable."

The most interesting part of the session was about Neddy's girlfriend Elizabeth. Kathy asked if I was going to get in touch with her, apropos of Neddy's birthday. I said no—it seemed too hard and too sad—that seeing her would rip it all open again.

Kathy wondered if it was particularly hard to see Elizabeth because of some mother-in-law/daughter-in-law interactions: competing for Neddy and blaming each other, which were emotions that would take place if he were alive. She asked me if I wanted to have a relationship with Elizabeth. I said, "Of course. There are few enough of us in the world who loved him." But really I thought, with anger, "I don't want *her*. I want *him*."

The next day I got a beautiful letter from Elizabeth. It was written on a card with a picture of Monet's Japanese footbridge and the water-lily pond at Giverny.

She said, in part, about her grief:

> Of course, sometimes I think it makes it seem like I didn't really love Ned—the fact that I can live without him. Really, the fact that I can live without him is due only to the fact that I once lived with him. My determination to live is out of an obligation to Ned and is rooted in my love for him . . .

On January 5, there was a snowstorm. Outside the window, snow blew horizontally. It fell heavily all morning and was expected to last the entire day.

I pulled logs out of their delivery sacks and stacked them on the andirons; the biggest in back, another in front, kindling linking the two, another log on top of the kindling. I crumpled newspaper and pushed it under the edifice, then made sure the flue was open. *Can't have another disaster like last time when all that smoke got into the room.*

Now, the scrape of a match. I touched the flame to the paper. The flame caught, eating into the newsprint. Soon the kindling was ablaze and the dry logs began to incinerate. I lay down on the rug, cupped my chin in my palms. The heat warmed my face.

I'm lying on the dark rug in the living room of my childhood home. The heat from the fire in the fireplace warms my face. I stare into the flames. There's commotion around me. Big brothers drape across the sofa, reading comic books. Big sister is doing her homework at Dad's desk in the back room. Mum's working in the kitchen, cooking dinner.

Daddy and the ritual of the fire. I am his helper. Together, we go to the cellar. Rickety, wooden steps leading down. Socks drying near the furnace. Whiskey bottle tucked behind the pipes. L.L. Bean boots with leather laces lie on the floor. Logs are piled up against the wall. I help to fill the leather log carrier. Dad hefts the carrier up the teetery stairs. I bring the kindling. Once upstairs, I watch Dad load logs into the fireplace; biggest in back, smaller in front, kindling linking the two. Soon heat scorches my wet wool snowpants hanging over the fire screen.

Later, outside, Dad cuts brush and drags it into a pile, ready for burning. I drag smaller branches across the snow, heave them onto the pile. "Stand back," Dad says. He sloshes kerosene from a gurgling can onto the nest of wood, and throws on a lighted match. The kerosene ignites with a whomp. Flames appear. The tender bark on the sticks starts to curl and run with liquid. Sap hisses. Smoke rises. The snow under the fire sizzles as it melts.

Now the wood burns steadily. Flames leap up toward the darkening sky. Steadily we work together, pulling branches through the snow and feeding them into the flames. When we turn away from the blaze to get new fuel, our faces become chilled. As the fire matures, we tug partially burned branches out of it and throw them back into the center of the conflagration.

Finally, there is nothing left but a patch of glowing coals ringed with ashes. Dad rakes the coals, sending up a shower of sparks into the night air. He makes sure that there is plenty of snow surrounding the still-glowing embers. We pick up our tools and head for the glowing lights of home.

The blazing wood snapped. I awoke out of my reverie to see andirons shaped like owls with glass orbs for eyes. The eyes shimmered with an oily flicker as they reflected the flames dancing behind them. I was staring into the fireplace in my apartment in New York City.

My father died eleven days before Neddy was born. I didn't even acknowledge the enormity of his death at the time. It would have been hard to do, because we moved to a new apartment— this one—three days before he died, and Martha was a rambunctious twenty-one-month-old, so I was busy. Anyway, I didn't know how to grieve then. I just called forth the old WASP reserve—and didn't cry, and kept a stiff upper lip, and drank more . . .

Now I reflected that I had eventually accepted my father's death, just as I had accepted my mother's. The process did take place, no matter how impeded by alcohol, repression. Would I get to the point where I could think of Neddy without pain? Without anger? Was I without anger, now, at my father? Not completely, but the rage I felt a few years before in the depths of therapy was gone. The old tenderness that was there before I acknowledged the hurt had not returned—but I felt a forgiveness and a distance I had never known before.

We shared so much, and adored each other so. I even looked like him. "Daddy with braids," was the way someone put it. To have that gentle, big man—my strong football-player father—sicken and die was more than I could take at the time. So I numbed out. I sat in the front pew at his funeral, feeling nothing, looking at the brocaded cover on the coffin and feeling nothing, hung over and feeling nothing, having to sit down because I felt dizzy—my "condition," you see, pregnant with Neddy—but really hung over, and feeling nothing.

A few days before Neddy's birthday, I developed a fever and aches in every joint.

I lay in bed for long periods, thinking, musing, *He is dead.* I was too sick to get up and run away from that thought. *He is dead.* I was glad that I had seen the body. A friend had told me that when her son had died, her daughter had begged and begged to see the body, but, because she herself couldn't stand to, she wouldn't let her. One mustn't be hard on oneself—we do the best we can at the moment. I'm glad I saw his body—it was hard enough, having seen it, to know it is true . . .

The night before Neddy's birthday I dreaded going to sleep, because I'd have to wake up to the knowledge that he was dead. I wondered what Ned was thinking; he must be in agony, too. It was impossible to call him and ask for or give comfort, share some sorrow.

When the day dawned, I lit a lonely candle in memory of Neddy. A pouring rain had washed away all the snow. I was still weak from the flu and was glad I hadn't driven up to the graveyard as I had planned. A huge and exquisite bouquet of snapdragons, delphinium, tulips, daisies, carnations was delivered to my door, a present I sent to myself.

The autumn before the winter that Neddy was born, my brother-in-law lost an election, Martha had her first eye operation at the Manhattan Eye and Ear Hospital, Ned and I saw "Cav" and "Pag" and *Beyond the Fringe*. We were into the Phoenix Theater, polo at the Armory, the Brauhaus on 86th Street, Giovanni's Restaurant.

I brought you forth in pain. Oh, the pain. I remember that night you were born. I woke up at 2:00 A.M. and we went to the hospital. "I'm going to put you in the twilight zone," the doctor said—the pain was so bad (were you a breech birth?), he didn't want me to remember. But the drug didn't work, and I remembered it all, up until the moment they knocked me out completely with anesthesia.

I woke up and there you were. I had a moment of shock—a reaction from the anesthesia?—a moment of confusion. Then I focused. You were so little and red and bloody, with a funny, scrunched-up face. A boy. A son. It was 10:00 A.M. You weighed six pounds eleven ounces, and measured nineteen and one-half inches long. Your father didn't see you until you were put in your crib in the nursery a few minutes later. They didn't let fathers in the delivery room then.

I still have the tiny blue and white bracelet you wore in the hospital. I still have your baby clothes—and Martha's—in a box. I still have your hair from your first haircut, and your baby teeth that you put under the pillow.

Did the doctor have to reach in and turn you around? Did he feel your little foot, or your bottom, or your face? Did he move your head so it pointed the right way, down the passageway? Did the soft bones of your head bend as you slid through the crushing gate? Did he pull you as I pushed? Did he use forceps? Did he turn you to get your shoulders out? What did your umbilical cord look like? The afterbirth? Did that moment of shock when I saw you in the delivery room make me wonder if somehow I didn't love you as much as Martha, with whom I'd fallen in love at first sight? Did it make me overcompensate all your life?

I remember holding you for the first time, in my hospital bed. You were wrapped up tight, swaddled in a bundle. Your father and I

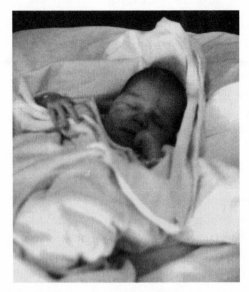

"You were . . .
swaddled in a bundle."

opened the blanket, checked out your hands and feet, counting your fingers and toes to make sure they were all there.

We came home a week after you were born. By then you'd been circumsized. I'm sure it hurt. People didn't believe babies felt pain then.

For a while, your eyes were blue. Later they changed to hazel. At first you didn't smile a real smile, only rictus smiles with burps.

At one month, you weighed eight pounds, fifteen ounces, and were twenty-one and one-half inches long. I took you to see my maternal grandmother, Granny. She was in her house on Seventy-eighth Street. Gampy had died at the age of ninety-seven the year before. Granny couldn't speak because she'd had a stroke. I remember how she stared at you—it was frightening. There was something horrible about her frozen face, one eye pulled down. She was holding a shell-like Silly Putty egg in her hand. I had given it to her one day when I brought Martha to visit. She clutched it for two years after she went to the nursing home. I never saw her again after that day I took you there. I couldn't bear to visit her. She was my grandmother Edith, for whom I was named. I have run away from a lot of things in my life.

You were completely weaned at three months.

At six months, you were baptized at the church where your funeral was.

Lilly, the governess who was hired by my parents when I was born and who stayed on until I was in college, was still alive when you were born. I called her Yoyo when I was too young to pronounce "Lilly" correctly, and after that everyone called her Yoyo. She died the next year at eighty-seven years old. Another unacknowledged blow, and someone I had to mourn twenty years later.

Now I'm looking at the photo albums. Awwww. What a cute little squinched-up face. Everyone came to see you. Here's you getting a bath in the sink. You're frowning that little frown newborns wear.

This was your first time outdoors, in the fancy blue English carriage with a seat across the end for Martha.

Here's a picture of Martha with you lying across her lap. She didn't want to touch you with her hands. Was she afraid of hurting you? When you learned to sit up, Martha got more friendly—or less scared.

Here's your cousin Dossy holding you. Oh, you're getting to be a big boy now.

Your father and I played "Patty Cake" with you and rode you on our foot reciting, "Ride a Cock Horse" and "This is the way the Farmer's Ride, Hobbledy Hoy, Hobbledy Hoy," and played "This Little Pig Went to Market," twiddling each tiny toe.

To commemorate Neddy's birthday, Martha and her friends went to a place in Golden Gate Park near the buffalo paddock and planted a cherry tree. There Martha received a testimonial from a representative of the park. It said, "The San Francisco Recreation and Park Department presents this certificate to Martha Davis to affirm the planting of a memorial tree Prunus Species at Golden Gate Park in loving tribute to Edward S. Davis Jr." The tree was a cherry. Its seeds were grown in Osaka, Japan, the sister city to San Francisco.

On the night of Neddy's birthday I had dinner with Elizabeth. "We all had denial," I said. "Everyone. Neddy most of all."

Elizabeth replied, "I know you thought I did, but it was ignorance, not denial. Ignorance about serious illness. You were the one who saw it coming," she added. "You deserve the least guilt."

"My therapist says you and I probably have a complicated relationship—like that of a mother-in-law and daughter-in-law, passing blame and guilt back and forth and competing for Neddy."

*"Oh, you're getting
to be a big boy now."*

"Are you angry at me?" Elizabeth burst out.

"Yes," I said, "and I'm angry at the doctors, and his father, and his landlord, and Neddy, and his boss, and myself, and anybody else who could have done something but didn't."

Later, my therapist Kathy said I had done a good job at dinner. She congratulated me for not protecting or taking care of Elizabeth (much), and for talking about myself and my feelings.

Kathy promised that someday I would have the perspective to see how Neddy and Elizabeth were struggling to define themselves, and how a life-threatening illness just didn't fit in. I would come to know that Neddy chose Elizabeth *because* of her traits— that he didn't *want* someone who would coddle him. Witness his behavior about his heart operation. It helped to get Kathy's reading that there was a *system,* an interaction going on, and that my blame of Elizabeth—not my rage, which was part of the mourning process—and my blame of myself were the same thing. If I cut myself off from Elizabeth, I would be cutting myself off from myself and postponing my mourning.

Was the sadness I felt after dinner engendered by the knowledge that I was forging a new relationship with Elizabeth that *left out* Neddy? Maybe that was what made it so chilling.

CHAPTER ELEVEN

As a boy, Neddy had an infectious, bubbly laugh and a piping, high voice. His straight, silky blond hair was worn in a bowl style with a bang over his forehead. He had a cute little button nose and a grin that curled his mouth straight up at the corners in a U. He was thin, friendly, nervous, lively, spunky, and, when he learned to talk, had an endearing way of mispronouncing words. "Just a liddle," "last ob all," "I will gib you," "he had aten up the last bite," and "roast beast," instead of "roast beef" are examples of some of his fractured English. He was quite mischievous and liked to see how far he could go without getting stopped. He loved to be cuddled and held. Quick to cry—this lasted well into his teens—he became quite frustrated if he couldn't immediately accomplish something. He was high-strung and bit his fingernails.

My husband, a new lawyer pushing hard, worked late almost every week night. I was lonely and burdened by the sometimes boring and exhausting, although rewarding, task of bringing up children.

Reading aloud was often a peaceful refuge after a busy day. In the evenings Martha and Neddy would snuggle up next to me on the sofa and we would delve into *The Story of Ping*, about a little duck who lived on a "wise-eyed boat on the Yangtze River," Ferdinand the bull, who just wanted to sit down and smell the flowers,

Babar the elephant and his family, and Pierre, the little boy in Maurice Sendak's *The Nutshell Library* who was cured of his defiant habit of declaring, "I don't care!" by being eaten by a lion. For a special treat, we would read a book my mother had written about a thin old lady who lived at the top of a high, high, terribly high building and loved her puffin Paul and sunflowers, or another one about the teeniest weeniest teeny teeny teeny weeny weeny weeny little dog in all the world, who one day started to GROW.

Before the children got old enough to go to school, we had our daily routine in the neighborhood. We went to a nearby playground in Central Park, where Martha and Neddy played on the swings and slides and seesaws or rode their tricycles, or to the statue of Alice in Wonderland or the zoo. We did errands. The "peapod store" was a local grocery where a friendly employee gave Neddy fresh peapods as a treat. Neddy would unzip the pod, pulling down the delicate little string on its edge, peel it back, and gobble up the peas. He also savored plums, his favorite fruit.

When the children were a little older, I and several other mothers started a small play group which rotated among our apartments. Ned made a table with benches and the children worked there with sewing cards or construction paper, paste, scissors, and glue, or used stamps and a stamp pad to make designs. Martha and Neddy began to have a circle of friends, who were the children of our adult friends.

Practically every weekend we drove out of the city to Ned's parents' farm on Pocono Road in Brookfield. My mother-in-law was a children's book author. I had read her books as a teenager in my "horse-crazy" stage. My father-in-law was a busy lawyer. They welcomed me into the family with great warmth and hospitality.

My father-in-law owned a herd of black Angus cattle. We were never at the farm for the annual slaughtering, but often partook of the "home-grown" beef that filled the freezer. When I first came to the farm, an ancient donkey and an ancient horse still occupied stalls at the barn, but they soon died. Chickens laid eggs, which had to be gathered each morning.

My mother-in-law, a hearty, enthusiastic woman of great intelligence and talent who wrote her books in a tiny, one-room house in the woods and had a phenomenal memory for classics, which she

". . . or to the statue of Alice in Wonderland . . ."

quoted voluminously, died suddenly at age fifty-one after we had been married a year and a half. It was a devastating blow. My father-in-law was single for the next few years, so we saw a lot of him.

Ned's five younger brothers and sisters, most of whom were fully grown, also came often to Brookfield, except for one of his sisters, who lived in Japan.

The autumn before Neddy was born, Ned and Martha and I moved into our own house on the farm. We were happy to have the privacy. Across Pocono Road there was a railroad spur and at night we could hear the soothing clack-clacking of trains passing by. In the spring, as the children grew older, we gathered frogs' eggs from a swampy area near the railroad tracks. We put them in a big jar of water and watched, fascinated, as they grew into tadpoles. Fresh green skunk cabbage leaves pushed up through the ground near an adjacent brook, heralding the change of the season. Soon rhubarb sprouted and I cooked it up with lots of sugar for a bitter, delicious dessert. Lilac and forsythia bushes bloomed near the house and clusters of crocuses and daffodils dotted the lawn. At Easter time, the children searched the long grass under blossoming apple trees for dyed eggs and presents that we had hidden. Peonies opened their large pink flowers and we gathered armfuls to wrap in wet newspaper for the trip back to the city. It was plowing and planting time. Wild fox kits were born and thrived in a den in the lower fields.

In summer, the cattle chewed constantly in the green fields along the river and grew fat. Violets and jack-in-the-pulpit bloomed in the woods. Fields of corn and rye grew tall in the sun. The smell of clover and new-mown grass hung in the air. My vegetable garden, in which were planted corn, squash, pumpkins, beets, carrots, sugar peas, tomatoes, and zinnias, marigolds, and cornflowers, required hoeing and weeding. Once a summer the cattle had to be moved from one field to another. Usually a cow escaped and galloped around, sometimes straight through the vegetable garden, until it was herded in with the others. We played tennis on my father-in-law's court and swam in his pool. Neddy paddled with a bright yellow Styrofoam bubble on his back. We cooked hamburgers and hot dogs on the grill. Friends or members of my family came to visit. Soon, however, my mother came alone, as my father died about a year after my mother-in-law did.

In the fall, we harvested the vegetables before the first hard frost, picking green tomatoes still attached to their vines and leaving them in the shelter of the garage to ripen slowly. We hauled pumpkins and Indian corn to New York. We put away outdoor furniture and stored the lawn mower. It was kite-flying weather. We husked the cattle's feed corn, cleaned the house and battened down the hatches.

The cows lived in the barnyard in the winter. My husband chopped wood, worked in his shop in the garage, and we tobogganed and sledded with the children. We studied the Burpee seed catalog and relished filling out our order form. We enjoyed word games, charades, and cowboy pool at night in my father-in-law's house. He played the piano by ear, and was an infectiously enthusiastic singer, so we joined in energetic renditions of Cole Porter songs and Broadway show tunes. We bought live evergreen trees, used them inside for our Christmas trees, and planted them outside by the driveway to screen us from the road.

Neddy loved the farm. He especially loved my father-in-law's dog, a Labrador retriever. Neddy would drape himself over Spinney's black back, just hanging there, sometimes with his feet off the ground. Spinney would stagger a little, but hold his ground. The first writing I have of Neddy's is about Spinney: Neddy was in third grade, and he wrote, "The Day i cried. Onc upon a time i had a dog and loved him and he was 5 years old and he died when he was 7." Neddy helped his father with chores and rode on farm vehicles, such as the stone boat, a wooden sled used for hauling stones out of the fields. Neddy and Martha started tending their grandmother's grave in the graveyard on the sandy hill in Brookfield with their father at an early age.

"Onc upon a time i had a dog."

It sounds idyllic, but there was a problem casting its shadow over everything.

Although I didn't know it, and neither did anyone else, I was alcoholic. Increasingly, I was handicapped in everything I did. The progressive symptoms of what I now believe to be a genetic disease were increasing: denial—I simply could not let myself or anyone else know what was happening, and yet it was searingly evident that I was in deep trouble; shame—I crossed the street to avoid old friends; isolation—I didn't want to see people or go places; and, of course, the ingestion of alcohol in increasing amounts. I had gained a good forty pounds of bloat and felt terrible about my body. I began to be inconsistent with the children, depending on my physical condition: if I was suffering from a hangover, I found their piercing voices—especially Neddy's, because it was shrill—almost unbearable. I began to develop a nasty temper. If I was slightly drunk or high I could be effusively affectionate, and I thought I was enormously funny. Increasingly, it was difficult to show up for events, as I was fearful of people. And, while we both drank daily, as had our parents, my husband was not amused. We were totally ignorant about alcoholism, its symptoms, and the fact that it is not a moral weakness. I tried desperately to "be a good person," but I felt like the worst creature in the world. It was increasingly difficult to do my job as wife and mother. I did not know about the fatal nature of the disease.

I was hospitalized twice, both times for disguised reasons. The alcoholism was never addressed by name on my medical record, although I clearly was affected by the drug—my liver was enlarged. The two hospitals I entered did not at the time have alcoholism units, and alcoholism was considered, even by doctors, a shameful diagnosis, something to be hidden.

While I was in the hospital the second time, Ned hired a wonderful Irish woman named Miss Connor to work for us as a housekeeper five days a week, and when I got out, I started seeing a psychiatrist. For the next five years the doctor and I discussed my drinking. I was secretly relieved when he concentrated on unearthing its underlying causes. At that time most health professionals didn't understand the nature of the disease; they didn't know that therapy generally doesn't work until the patient stops drinking, and discovering underlying causes doesn't relieve the symptoms. Although I didn't land in the hospital again, and on some level was able to fool myself that I was getting better, the truth was that I continued to get sicker.

When Neddy was four, the government decided to extend a highway directly through the middle of my father-in-law's farm. The land had to be sold. This was devastating news to my father-in-law, for he had lived there for more than thirty years. However, he was now remarried and began to plan a new life in another state. We bought land farther north, in New Milford, Connecticut.

The land was all ours, which was exciting. It consisted of both wooded sides of a valley with a stream at the bottom of the valley. We fell in love with it.

First, we needed to find water. I had discovered that I had a talent for dowsing, and toted my forked fruit-tree stick with me everywhere I went, even when we visited friends for the weekend, finding forgotten wells and hidden sewer systems. Now I walked our land near the site we had chosen for a house, holding my forked stick in front of me, marching methodically in a crisscross pattern. Near the top of the hill, the stick turned violently in my hands and pointed down, scraping skin off my palms so they bled. Consequently, a well was drilled, and water flowed in at a respectable rate. Eventually a prefabricated dwelling called a Deck House was erected.

As we moved in, I was severely incapacitated. I was at the stage of bargaining with alcohol: giving up hard liquor and drinking beer or wine, going on the wagon, trying to manipulate the disease, struggling to appear normal.

My husband was very angry and unhappy. At first he tried not speaking to me. And, silent or not, it was agony for us to be alone together, so we invited his sister to visit us practically every weekend. At this time I tried desperately to maintain the fiction that I was happy and interested in my life, but the actuality was that I found it increasingly difficult to get up in the morning, or to go out during the day, or to perform basic duties such as meeting with the children's teachers. Ned cooked breakfast and took the children to their school buses. My mother took me on a trip, and other people tried to help me, but I perceived some of their efforts as accusation, and friends got dropped by the way. This period was marked by repeated new starts, where I would go on a diet, give up booze, get up early in the morning, try to find a hobby. However, eventually these reforms failed and I always found myself in a new and more serious phase. Ned's ire grew, his disapproval, his unhappiness, and my defensiveness, yes, belligerence. It all happened gradually. Today I can feel compassion for both of us, lost as we were in ignorance.

Finally, soon after a miserable Christmas in 1969, my husband moved out for good, and I was alone with the children. Because of the looming shadow of my alcoholism, Ned and I had never addressed or even recognized what might have been problems in our marriage brought on by differences in our personalities and temperaments. I drank for another three years.

The children were ten and eight when we divorced. For many years, Neddy longed for us to reunite. He simply couldn't bear that his parents had split up permanently.

I received custody of the children. They soon settled into a routine of weekend and vacation visits with Ned. But my sadness, shame, and sense of failure over the end of the marriage lasted a long time.

The structure of our days was defined by school, extracurricular activities, homework, and leisure time. Even when he was very young, Neddy loved jingles and games, and constantly wanted to play checkers or dominoes or slapjack. When he got older, he liked card games. He also loved working with a Spirograph and Etch-a-Sketch, and, older, sat for hours at the dining room table doing 10,000-piece jigsaw puzzles, a whiz at putting them together by color, shape, and size; patiently turning, turning the pieces around and around, scrutinizing them. Still older, he loved chess.

He threw a rubber ball against the kitchen wall and caught it endlessly in his baseball mitt, pegging line drives and scooping up grounders. He worked hard to get a good pocket in his mitt, and rubbed neat's-foot oil into it to make it flexible.

Dressed in white pants and a blue blazer and diminutive rep tie, Neddy was the ring bearer for my niece in her wedding. He was very insulted to learn that the real ring was in the pocket of the best man, and he was only carrying a fake, which was sewn to the little ceremonial pillow he held so carefully on his solemn and measured trip down the aisle.

He and Martha liked Mad Libs, where the reader fills in blanks in a printed story with inappropriate words, and howled with laughter at the hilarious results. He also had many jokes with Miss Connor, many laughs, many giggles, many yucks. Neddy loved jokes. He accused me of not having a sense of humor. He loved to laugh all-out, from the belly, real guffaws. Many people who wrote me after he died mentioned his laugh.

"Neddy loved all animals."

Neddy loved all animals. He especially loved my sister's cats, Boy-Boy and Girl-Girl, and her dog, Willie. He adored Coolie Dog, a large standard poodle in Bermuda, where we visited my husband's relatives, and Noir, a big black Newfoundland owned by my cousin, and Askari, the German shepherd owned by our English friends. He never owned a dog of his own, even though he longed for one. We didn't feel it was fair to a big dog (which was what he wanted) to keep it in the city. Later, when the "pooper scooper" law came in and a dog's owner had to pick up the dog's excrement and dispose of it, he was glad he didn't own a dog in the city.

Neddy's birthday parties were memorable. They always included Spider Web, a unique game involving multicolored yarns stretched crisscross between pieces of furniture in the living room. The object was to follow your own yarn through the tangled web

". . . double-chocolate cake . . ."

and find the present hidden at the end. We always played Pin the Tail on the Hippo, Musical Chairs, and ate scrumptious double-chocolate cake with elaborate theme decorations.

One summer Martha and Neddy and I went to Nantucket for a month. Neddy loved leaping and skidding down the cliffs to the beach each day, jumping on a trampoline, bicycling to the windmill and the harbor, going to the Penny Candy Shop, picnicking on the beach at night with friends. A decomposing whale washed ashore and we couldn't get the stench out of our noses. Neddy bought a rope bracelet, a wristlet like sailors used to wear, and wore it without taking it off for the next five years until it was slimy and stinky. I let the children "stay up all night." Actually they fell asleep by midnight, but they had permission to stay up all night if they wanted to. We had a race on the beach with "sports cars." Mounds of molded sand formed the cars around the seated race car drivers. Frisbees made good steering wheels.

Neddy attended kindergarten at the school connected with the church where his funeral was. At school he learned about seeds and germination, telling time, and the seasons of the year. There was rest, singing, "roof," which was riding tricycles on the schoolhouse roof, and, best of all, going home.

After two years of kindergarten, Neddy entered first grade at Collegiate School, a boy's school his father had also attended. Neddy was old for his class since he had a January birthday, but he was smaller than most of his classmates and struggled with the work. Consequently, he repeated second grade, which was hard on him because he had to make a whole new set of friends.

In second grade he was interviewed by a psychologist because he was disruptive in the classroom and his teachers suspected emotional difficulties relating to the breakup of the marriage. At that time he tested with a low rating in reading comprehension and came across as naive, immature, and somewhat inattentive. He had some fears he would be abandoned, but they were not overwhelming. A great deal of remedial work in reading was recommended, as he was falling behind his class.

I remember my interview with the same doctor. She suggested I get help, too. I assured her I was seeing a psychiatrist. I was humiliated that she thought something was wrong with me. Actually, I was drinking and trying to cover it up. I was also trying desperately to help myself, to help Neddy, and to be a responsible parent.

Neddy was tested further and judged to have attention-deficit hyperactivity disorder. He had symptoms: fidgeting with his hands and feet, squirming, difficulty waiting his turn in a group, blurting out answers to questions before they were completed, difficulty following directions and sustaining attention, shifting between uncompleted activities, not listening when someone was speaking to him.

In short, Neddy suffered from impulsivity and distractibility. This was very difficult on him, I am sure, and for the people around him. He could be irritating.

The symptoms of attention-deficit hyperactivity disorder are usually present from birth. Parents often blame themselves, but, according to an article in the New York *Times,* "The precise causes of the syndrome are not known. Birth complications and head injuries are rarely involved, although some studies suggest that prenatal exposure to alcohol or cigarettes may increase the risk. Nor is the condition caused by allergies or sensitivities to food additives or refined sugar; only in a few cases does avoiding these substances result in a 'normal' child.

"Rather, the problem seems to be a neurological disorder that is often hereditary and that involves the brain mechanisms that regulate attention and impulse control."

Certainly I had drunk alcohol when I was pregnant—including the night Neddy was born—and had smoked more than a pack of cigarettes a day. After Neddy died, I talked to the pediatrician who had first examined him hours after he was born and who had been his doctor throughout his childhood. He said, "Neddy had no signs of damage from your drinking. Blaming yourself is simply not appropriate." I wondered, though, if doctors of that era were simply not trained to look for such symptoms.

Neddy started taking small doses of the stimulant drug Ritalin, which increased his concentration. He also took Benadryl at night to help him go to sleep. Later I worried that the Ritalin had caused him to be shorter than he might have been otherwise—it sometimes has the effect of stunting growth. His adult height was about 5′6″.

He was a hard worker and was always making progress. Anyone who had ever worked with him described him as willing, industrious, diligent, and good-natured.

One can trace the improvement of Neddy's organizational, spelling, and writing skills through a sampling of his letters from five years of summer camp, starting when he was ten:

Dear Mummy on the bus I met a freind which I doent no his name. I am in North glenuya my cabin. My first night in Kieve was *great!* We put our cloath on shelves and i made my bed almost all by myself. I am looking forward to the next 2 months. By it is launch time so i have to go by lots of love love xxx oooo Neddy

Dear Mummy,

I am sorry to say but i will not be writing you a lot because i am haveing so much fun and i am haveing so much fun the gong is about to ring which means it is activeite time so by love Neddy. Write soon.

Dear Mummy,

How are you I am fine it is so hot you would die. nothing mouch is happening so I do not have mouch to say last night we did skits and

I was the star of the show. There is nothing else to say so Bye. Lots of love Neddy.

Dear Mummy,

today is sunday and we have inspection. I will try to call but if I can't here's a letter. a couple of days ago I had to tump a canoe but I could not do it that way so I tried it a harder way and it was really easy so I carried the canoe 2 miles the hard way. I am going on a trip for 2 weeks starting the 7th and it ends the 21st. I just got back from lunch and I got bitten by a dog on my right forfinger and that is why I can't write very well. Well there isn't much more to say so bye love Neddy.

From a camp for dyslexic students:

Dear Mummy,

Today is Sunday and we have to write letters. Daddy came up yesterday and we went out to lunch, then went to Falling Water. A picture of it is on the cover of this card. It is a house that is built over a water fall and was built by Frank Lloyd Wright. Today is very hot and I can barely write this letter because I am so hot. One reason I am so hot is because I was just playing football and I ran too much. Tomorrow I am going water skiing and I am going to try slolum again . . .

A cartoon on a birthday card Neddy sent me when he was twenty-six years old shows a cat typing a letter which reads, "hHapKpY BIRCt/hd az!" In Neddy's handwriting inside the card: "Typical of a dyslexic cat. He must take after me. If he does he is a pretty special cat!"

In sixth grade Neddy was officially diagnosed with dyslexia, and it became evident that he couldn't keep up with the work at Collegiate School anymore, even with tutoring. Neddy and his father and I looked at several less demanding schools in New York. Neddy was turned down by one, and we didn't like the other. Although we were divorced, Ned and I talked often and worked as a team with the schools and doctors on making this decision. We went jointly with Neddy to look at several other boarding schools before settling on a small coed day- and boarding school that wasn't too far from Ned's weekend house in Connecticut and where he could get the extra help he needed in a disciplined and supportive environment.

Throughout his life, Neddy felt on some level that he was sent away to boarding school because he did something wrong. He never forgave us for "making" him go away. Even though he liked Indian Mountain School and as an adult became a recruiter for it, he continued to have the same nagging emotional response. I could never quite convince him that we had had his best interests at heart.

Neddy was a student at Indian Mountain School for three years from the ages of thirteen to sixteen years old. He was homesick at first, but he worked very hard and became much more proficient at language skills. He played goalie on the ice hockey team and wing on the soccer team, and made good friends. At the end of his final year he won a prestigious award called the Schutte Prize for diligence and improvement. At his death, the certificate for the award was framed and hung prominently on the wall of his apartment.

After he died, I got a letter from Indian Mountain's alumni/nae director:

". . . many of his friends have called or written to ask for more details. They were very shocked and saddened to learn of his death. He certainly had many good friends at IMS who cared a great deal for him.

". . . Indian Mountain School is fortunate to have been able to count Neddy as one of its own."

CHAPTER TWELVE

It was February and the filthy snow in the streets was frozen. I took the subway downtown for a therapy session. My therapist, Kathy, and I agreed that Bill had probably used the other woman as a "hook," to pull him out of the relationship. I didn't believe now that he had been sleeping with her.

My interest in doing my big painting revived. I made small sketches of the boats, and worked on them with colored pencils, trying out different color schemes. I taped them to the wall of Neddy's room, then fastened together sixteen 14″ × 17″ tracing paper sheets to make one huge piece of paper, and drew my final giant sketch on it. The next step seemed exhausting, so I let the project lapse again.

By the time Neddy graduated from Indian Mountain School in 1979, I had been sober for six years and was working in a publishing company.

When I finally asked for help with my drinking problem and became willing to receive it, the urge to drink miraculously disappeared.

With the aid of newfound friends and an informed doctor, I was able to gradually diminish and then discontinue the massive dose of Valium that I had been ingesting under the psychiatrist's orders. It was a harrowing withdrawal, and my motor responses were affected. The new doctor said I had sustained damage to my cerebellum.

Frankly, I didn't care. The world seemed new, and everything was fresh. I felt a great liberation as I began to learn about the disease from which I had suffered so long in ignorance.

Martha and Neddy entered into my recovery powerfully. They learned about alcoholism, and became experts at passing on suggestions, quoting slogans, and generally monitoring my condition.

The world was a frightening place, and I was still very sick. I often wore a raincoat in public, night and day, summer and winter, for about a year after I stopped drinking, because I was so self-conscious.

However, it was wonderful to be able to show up at the children's field days and for conferences with their teachers without having to worry about covering up my boozy breath with mouthwash. But it wasn't easy at first to live in the world without drugs. I had enormous fear about everything, including crossing the street. My perception of the city was faulty—splintered. I wasn't sure how or if the West Side connected to the East Side, for instance. The looming buildings in Midtown seemed almost alive.

The first summer I was sober the children and I spent a month on Long Island. We were like survivors from a shipwreck, washed up on the beach. We ate fresh fruits and vegetables and swam in the ocean. The bloat began to fall off me. A smile of relief began to wreathe my face. The human organism is remarkable, given a chance.

When we returned to the city, I got a job working as a volunteer in the office of a neighborhood newspaper. I emptied wastepaper baskets and typed up memos. The difficulty was in getting there on time. My nervous system was messed up, and my sleeping habits, after years of ingesting alcohol, which is a depressant drug, plus the prescription drugs Valium, Seconal, and chloral hydrate, were very erratic. I continued to carry Valium in my purse for about six months, just in case I couldn't endure something and had to pop one. I never did. About ten months later, I got an entry-level job at a children's book publisher, where I continued to work for twelve years.

I had never worked full time before, and I loved it. I soaked up information about children's stories—structure, pacing, vocabulary; and artwork—composition, theme, design; and tools of the trade—galleys, proofs, chromalins. Behind my facade, I lived a secret life. When I descended each evening into the subway to go home, I peered surreptitiously at the half-empty pint bottle of whiskey that someone placed on the steps every night—seemingly to share with a friend who would soon come along. Almost humorously, I imagined myself writhing on the concrete floor in my business suit, sucking on the bottle, or licking the filthy floor to salvage a few drops.

Before I was hired by the publishing company, I told the personnel director I was a sober alcoholic. Her matter-of-fact reaction ("Well, maybe you can help us around here. After all, 7 percent of the population has the disease.") and my subsequent employment was a big step forward in combating my shame. Over the years at the company, I worked my way up from editorial assistant to assistant editor, editor, then senior editor.

In Neddy's last year at Pomfret, after seven years of working, my first children's book was published. It was written "on staff," which meant I didn't get paid. I was thrilled anyway.

My mother had always been the children's book writer in the family, but she had been dead for two years. Suddenly stories poured out of me. One year I wrote ten books. One of the first was *Ned's Number Book.* It was a counting book about a little boy named Ned who went to the park with his mother and ate plums, his favorite fruit. A year later, *Martha's House* came out. I wrote my first fifteen or so books on staff, and discovered that I liked writing nonfiction as well as fiction. Some of the books were formula jobs under pseudonyms, but I enjoyed crafting the stories, and I think I always brought imagination to the task.

The turning point came when I was asked to write and illustrate a companion to *Pat the Bunny,* for which I would actually get paid. I labored to invent a work which was modern and new, yet reflected the old and beloved. Illustrating proved especially difficult, but, as it turned out, I was able to bring a pleasing simplicity and unstudied quality to the art.

I traveled around the country to sign autographs. Although it was hard to overcome my innate shyness I found these trips fun and exciting. Autographing was a far cry from passing out in my apartment, and I thanked God every day.

Later when the publishing company I worked for wanted me to go back to writing for free, I refused. Other publishers were urging me to write for them, and I wanted to. My company threatened to fire me for breaking the conflict-of-interest clause in my employment contract if I wrote for another house under my own name. A lawyer said I should challenge them, but I was unwilling to, so I began to look for a new job. This was all very difficult for me. Eventually I decided to go out on my own. To date, I've written fifty-seven published children's books and illustrated twelve.

The best thing about writing—aside from earning a living—is having the opportunity to explore a broad range of personal interests. For me those interests range from Pompeii and ancient Egypt to sea otters, weather, farming, the circus, veterinary medicine, archeology, giant sea creatures. I've ridden to a fire in a fire chief's car, interviewed a milkman at 4:00 A.M., walked a beat with a police officer, counted whales for a scientific association, photographed a circus from the center ring. I've invented an alligator who watches videotapes, a boy who becomes invisible, and a "remembering game."

In September 1982, after his graduation from Pomfret, which he attended after Indian Mountain, I saw Neddy off for Beloit College in Wisconsin. He was nineteen.

Freshman Week was soon over. Informally it was called "Fuck Week" by the students—because that's what everyone did. Not Neddy. His relationship with Johanna was strong, unconsummated, and now, long-distance.

When I called him, someone answered the phone with, "Ned's Head Shop," which I found amusing, knowing Neddy and his fear of drugs. Gradually, he began to abandon his scruples about drinking. After some experimentation, he found he had a large capacity for booze. I warned him that high tolerance to alcohol can be an early sign of trouble.

Neddy seemed on top of the world. He was popular, and was making new friends. He was taking math, bio, chemistry, psychology, and was playing soccer, lifting weights, jogging. He looked

"... he seemed to qualify as a hunk."

wonderful and was bursting with health, strength, humor, competence. His longish hair was bleached gold on top by the sun. At last he seemed to qualify as a hunk.

Charlie, a friend from Pomfret, also attended Beloit, and they became very close. Both went out for varsity soccer, and both got on the team. They spent a lot of time together on vacations, too, because Charlie lived near us in New York.

About this time something happened which was to affect the whole family and had a bearing on Neddy's and my relationship over the next years. My ex-husband had remarried, and now he stopped paying me alimony although we had a legal contract. I sued him for the money. He sued me back. The bitter fight continued for seven years. Frightening, humiliating rounds of wranglings, depositions, and court appearances seemed endless. The suit was finally settled out of court. Goaded by circumstances to earn more money, I learned a great deal about taking care of myself. The lawsuit effectively ended my ex-husband's and my coparenting of our children, because our communication with each other ended then.

Neddy still pushed himself physically. When he reported to me from Beloit that he was running ten miles a day, I called Dr. K and then wrote Neddy a letter about the effects he could experience if he continued to run long distances. His heart could regurgitate blood, which might flood his lungs and cut off his air supply, causing heart failure. While it wouldn't kill him, it could be dangerous and frightening. I cautioned him about denial and reminded him about the role of denial in my own life when I was an active alcoholic. Even now, I still had to be constantly vigilant in combating it.

I didn't mail that letter. I knew I shouldn't be the one to impart such frightening information. I don't remember how this incident was resolved, but he did receive the information, for soon he wrote me:

Dearest Mother (Mom, Mum, Mummy, etc. Whatever you like best),

I finally have enough time to write you a good letter. Both the articles you sent me were very interesting especially the one about kids sucking tokens and you know I am always interested in the ups and downs of George Thomas Seaver.

. . . I am getting into very good shape (oops I propable [sic] shouldn't tell you this you might go tell a doctor and then lay me up in a hospital for a month). Sorry for the sarcasm but I have begun to be irritated about telling you how much exercise I do because you think I will have heart failure. It is the area that I am most proud of myself. Anyhow, I am running alot each day and I have put myself on a good lifting program. Now don't get all upset, Dr. G's tests say I am in fine shape and there should be no restrictions on me what so ever.

Not much more news here. Grades are O.K. C, C plus, B minus approx . . .

Neddy had switched cardiologists and was now a patient of Dr. G of New York City, who explained that the timing for the operation was tricky. There would be no benefit if surgery took place too soon, but if it were put off too long, the heart muscle would be damaged. He added that the condition was one of the "most forgiving" kinds of valve malfunction; the effects could be tolerated for a long time. Dr. Leonard offered to talk to me about any concerns I might have, and over the next five years until just before the operation took place, we conferred repeatedly.

Neddy wrote me from Beloit concerning his future plans. He was thinking of going into engineering, which would require a lot of math, a subject in which he was strong. He was considering entering a 3–2 program, which would mean three years at Beloit and then two years at another school, preferably one on the East Coast, before he got his B.A. degree. Then he planned to go to graduate school. If he didn't get a job as an engineer, he said, he could always fall back on teaching math or physics or a science at a high school or a preprep.

By this time, Bill had entered my life, and now our romance was blossoming. He spent more and more time at my apartment and began to spend the night. When Neddy first realized Bill was sleeping over, he bolted to his father's apartment and didn't come home for three days.

In the spring of freshman year, the Beloit soccer team went to England. They played Oxford and Southampton and visited Windsor Castle, Stonehenge, Stratford-on-Avon, and Westminster Abbey. It was a full-fledged cultural tour as well as a soccer tour.

Neddy was forming a pattern which I found upsetting: staying out all night without informing me. The first time it happened, he was home for vacation with some friends. We had dinner together but he was bored and uncommunicative. All he seemed to want to do was go to bars and meet girls.

Anyway, he didn't come home that night and neither did his friends. When he finally turned up the next day, I told him, "This is just unacceptable behavior. At school when you do this, it's probably O.K., but in New York it's just too dangerous. If you're going to live with me there's an important rule, and the rule is that you have to call, no matter what shape you're in, to tell me you plan to stay out all night."

"But I never sleep in my dorm." Neddy glared at me defiantly.

"I don't care. When you're home the rule is that you have to call."

"Well," he bellowed, "then I'm moving out!"

"O.K. Fine!"

"I'll live with my father and at college!" He'd given up calling his father "Daddy" because he thought it was too childish.

"O.K.," I stated, firmly, "but the rule when you're here is you have to call!"

"O.K.," he suddenly assented. "Then I'll abide by the rule."

In his sophomore year at Beloit, Neddy broke up with Johanna. When I visited him on campus, we talked about his relationship with girls. He came on strong, but when things got serious, he freaked out. He thought all they wanted was to marry him, and he didn't want to marry after experiencing Ned's and my relationship, he said.

After a year and a half at school, Neddy decided to take time off, live at home, and get a job. Soon he had landed a job as a messenger/receptionist/computer operator at a lithography company on Union Square and was living with me. He was twenty years old.

I could sense his relief at being home for a long stretch for the first time since sixth grade. He hung up the Indian bedspreads I'd bought for him at Azuma as well as a treasured poster of Tom Seaver pitching and a big cartoon of Abbott and Costello reciting their "Who's On First" routine. Once he had drawn his lines of independence, which meant he bought most of his own food and paid for his own phone, he could really relate to me. It was very gratifying; there was a tremendous sense of reunion.

Bill was on the scene more and more. Neddy liked him very much. A long-time teacher, Bill was a skillful mediator with Neddy, who planted his feet down over the dumbest things with me and would not budge—but when Bill shed light on the same subjects, Neddy listened. It was a blessed time, a busy time, a golden time.

The tranquility didn't last long. After eight months at home, Neddy suddenly quit his job and hastily left New York to be a camp counselor. He felt he'd been treated with contempt on the job. He wrote me that it was a learning experience, like burning your hand on a stove. Anyway, in a few months school would start again and he was now eager to go back.

Before the fall term started, however, Neddy received the news that his father wouldn't pay his tuition at Beloit anymore because he considered that Neddy was in trouble with drinking and felt that his grades were suffering. It was true that Neddy's grades had gone down a bit because of the transition to college, but I had been watching him carefully, and I didn't agree with his father's assessment. However, it was impossible to discuss the situation because of the lawsuit.

Neddy was extremely upset about having to leave Beloit and felt trapped by his dependency on his father for tuition money. He bitterly threatened to quit school altogether. I told him he could live at home if he wanted to go to a community or state college, but that he absolutely must finish his education. I urged him not to sever relations with his father. Eventually he applied to some schools nearer home and was accepted as a provisional student at Drew University in Madison, New Jersey.

That autumn he lived at home and commuted each day to Drew. I was apprehensive because he swore he would have no social life, play no sports, do nothing but cram to accomplish the Bs that his father required. This single-mindedness made me very nervous.

When I questioned him, Neddy assured me he wasn't going to isolate himself. He talked about working at the radio station at Drew and going to weekly movies there to combat loneliness.

Good things happened for me that fall, and once again it was a golden time. I went on National Public Radio to talk about one of my children's books. Neddy taped the show and had it playing at top volume when I came home from work. At the "New York is Book Country" fair on Fifth Avenue, I sat at a booth and signed copies of my book. Neddy stood next to me proudly.

Bill had moved in. He and Neddy got along well. They met for chats in the kitchen before their respective commutes.

I repeatedly wrote in my diary that I was worried about Neddy. He studied too long. If he wasn't studying, he was sitting in front of the TV. He was always in the apartment. He refused to have a balanced life. He was carrying his way of getting through "pressure systems" too far.

Bill was worried about Neddy, too. We were almost afraid to leave him alone when we went away for a weekend, because usually he didn't even go out. I took him to lunch and questioned him closely, and he said he was making friends at Drew, but it was hard not living on campus. Finally, I got in touch with the dyslexia doctor, who was able to give Neddy the support and encouragement he needed.

At last Neddy heard that he'd been accepted at Drew as a full student, to start in January. He ended up getting an A– on his Econ exam. He moved on campus.

After a few months, Neddy said his life was really in gear now. His studies were going well, he'd met a girl he liked and with whom he jogged each morning. For extracurricular activities, he hoped to do backstage work and take up soccer. He said he had screwed up at Beloit—his priorities were all wrong—and now he was on the right track.

About a year later, a frightening incident took place. Neddy cut himself falling off his bike. He neglected to take the antibiotics that were prescribed, and ended up in the hospital with a hugely swollen, infected arm. He also concealed his heart condition from the attending physician.

I lectured Neddy about taking responsibility and about self-destructiveness. He had to take care of himself, especially with his heart operation coming up soon.

We were both very aware of the impending operation. After recovering from the hospital incident, he came home for vacation. As he took his wet laundry down to the clothes dryer in the basement before going out for the evening, he stopped at the door, smiled humorously, and said, "I'll love you forever if you'll take my laundry out of the dryer." Then he paused, looked serious, and added, "I'll love you forever, anyway."

CHAPTER THIRTEEN

I crossed the street to Central Park. The February Winter Series ten-miler had just finished. The volunteers were taking down the clock and dismantling the finish line. Ragged chutes made of phosphorescent tape to channel the runners were still in place. Crumpled paper cups lay on the pavement. I passed the runners and limped, favoring my left leg, up to the reservoir track.

The lake was frozen. Black ice, lined with white cracks, stretched across it. A pressure ridge where new ice had formed paralleled the shore.

The temperature was eighteen degrees. I tightened the scarf across my face and curled my fingers, encased in thin glove liners, into fists inside my woolen mittens, then set off.

Birds clustered at the north end of the lake near a cut in the ice that led to the opposite shore. Herring gulls made up the majority of the flock. A few mallards floated among the gulls. The birds moved constantly, either dipping their heads rhythmically into the water, or flapping their wings, or taking off and flying, or landing with a splash. A great black-backed gull stood still on the edge of the ice near the flapping mob. It was huge compared to the other gulls.

I sat down on the granite wall beside the pumping station and pulled my sheepskin hat low over my eyes to cut the glare, jammed my clenched hands into my pockets.

A passerby heaved some hardened snow over the chain fence. A twang reverberated through the ice as the snow hit and splattered.

A few mallards floated near me in the open cut. The males had green iridescent heads and necks; the wing feathers of one of them hadn't folded back correctly, and a purple underfeather was exposed. The females had duller, mottled brown plumage. The ducks quacked nasally and chased each other, splashing. Their webbed feet were bright orange.

It was too cold to sit any longer. Getting up from my perch, I walked west on the track. I thought of something reassuring I'd read that morning about how universal guilt is in bereaved parents. The author urged readers not to deny it, but to try to limit thoughts beginning with, "If only." I mused that it was still easier for me to take on the guilt rather than to admit I was angry at Neddy or powerless over his death.

An approaching jogger laughed, drew to a halt, and spoke to me. "You're being followed," he said, pointing.

I glanced around. A squirrel was at my heels. "I guess it's hungry," I responded.

"Yeah. They forget where they hide their food," said the jogger, gearing up again and trotting away. The squirrel hopped to the edge of the path.

As I walked on again, paying attention as each booted foot met the track, I thought about the fact that we have no assurance that we will even live out the day. Past and future are dreams; all we have is awareness of the precious present moment.

In April of 1987, Neddy wrote me concerning his operation:

Dear Mummy,

So that it is easier for you, me and Martha to make plans, I think you should know that I am tentatively set to have surgery on my valve on June 10, and I will probably be in the hospital from June 7 to June 20.

Please note the following:

1. DO NOT CALL ME IMMEDIATELY to talk about this. If you have to talk to someone, talk to Bill, not me. Basically, I am afraid you will overreact and talk to me about how you are feeling.

2. I am not going to be at school this weekend and I have an exam and a presentation on Monday so if you have pertinent and useful information, I suggest you write me a letter.
3. If you want to give me something, you can donate blood in my name. I have "O+" and yours has to be the same for you to donate for me. Information concerning blood can be gotten at the enclosed phone number.
4. The valve is a pig valve which means that after the operation I will have no restrictions whatsoever. The operation is purely beneficial.

If you have questions, I suggest you hire a doctor to answer them, because neither my doctors nor I will answer any questions.

Love, Neddy

He had instructed Dr. G not to discuss his case with anyone, including me, because he wanted to be in charge of imparting information about it himself. I already knew this, as I had called Dr. Leonard and he had come on the line to say he couldn't talk—he had to respect Neddy's wishes—after all, Neddy was twenty-four years old—and that he would report to Neddy that I had called him. (He did.) I continued to talk to Dr. K behind Neddy's back.

I was very frightened about the operation, and had been for years. Death rates for heart surgery at that time were about 4.18 percent. The hospital Neddy was about to enter had one of the lowest death rates, but people did die from surgery. I almost expected it to happen. Looking back now, I wonder if this was part of my low self-esteem, or a charm to keep the gods on my side. Neddy knew I was scared, and it drove him crazy.

He had decided to move out of the apartment before the operation. "I'm going to the hospital and I don't know what's going to happen, and I want to be independent. I don't want to come back here to my childhood room," he said. After he made the decision to move out, he called three times and came home for lunch, all the way from New Jersey, ostensibly to pick up a book. While he was there, we had a talk about suicide. My therapist Kristina, whom I had started seeing after I quit my job, said the conversation couldn't have taken place without my giving him permission to move out first. Essentially, Neddy said he "understood" why some kids commit suicide, but that he wasn't suicidal. He said he felt that suicide was "the ultimate selfish act," and would hurt others immeasurably.

As always, when in a tight spot, Neddy acted erratically, and took it out on me. He stayed out all night. He had periods of not speaking to me. When he did speak to me, he was rude or withdrawn or angry at my obvious fears. For a while he wanted me to conceal the fact of the operation from other family members. His shame about it was so strong that he feared that this flaw in his body would make them consider him "weak."

When he actually appeared to pack up the furniture from his room, we had a wonderful visit. His excitement about moving and the future was infectious.

We got out our calendars and planned out the summer. Neddy would stay with Bill and me for a week after the operation, sleeping in Martha's room, and then, while I was away at a business convention in California, he would stay with his father. After that he'd visit a resort in Pennsylvania with Martha for a period of recuperation and eventually he'd start work again at the bookstore at Drew. He hoped to be on something he called the "semivarsity" soccer team at school in the fall.

Neddy moved heavy furniture and filled numerous large cartons, piling them in the hall. He carried them downstairs and loaded them in his car, came back for another enormous load. I accused him of terminal macho, especially since he was taking vasodilators now in preparation for surgery. He said that he always took on the hardest jobs of lifting at the bookstore because he had the most energy, and also because he was trying to prove there was nothing wrong with him. I rolled my eyes.

I made chicken sandwiches. As he ate, Neddy told me the pig valve would last fifteen years at the longest. He had chosen it because with it he wouldn't have to have any restrictions after the operation. "If I had the other kind of valve, a metal ball and base, maybe it would last longer, but I'd have to take anticoagulants every night so blood wouldn't clot on the metal. For all intents and purposes, I'd be a hemophiliac. With the pig valve I can do anything I want. Even skydive!"

"You'll be my point man?" he blurted out. Meaning would I organize the people who had offered to give blood? Now he had decided not to hide his condition and was accepting blood from family and friends. "You'll take charge?"

"Of course." Tears sprang to my eyes and almost brimmed over. There had been such tension between us. Now I could be point man, the soldier who goes first and takes the fire.

"With the pig valve," he repeated, "if I want to go parachuting or scuba diving, I can."

Later, I was glad he had chosen that kind of valve. Some batches of the metal ball and base variety proved defective. The device, known as the Bjork-Shiley 6-degree Convexo-Concave valve, fractured in more than 500 patients worldwide, killing two out of three.

I sat at the kitchen table and looked at him. I couldn't bear that he was going to be cut open. His face was so earnest and smudged, and he seemed so tired. His lazy eye was "off," looking crooked. The top of his head as he bent over was pink and vulnerable through his thinning hair. I allowed myself the thought that I couldn't bear never to see him again.

The next week a friend came over and met with Neddy and me for three and a half hours of straight talk about heart valve operations. My friend had had three of them—as Neddy would have to, and more, in his lifetime. Neddy heard all kinds of details like how they shave you from neck to feet. He was open and curious, and spoke about his fear of not surviving.

"My blood rotted in the airport," Martha said over the phone from California. She sounded angry and upset. She had decided not to come East for the operation but planned to go to Pennsylvania with her little brother afterwards. For now, she had expected to be represented by her blood.

"What? What do you mean?" I gasped.

"I told you," Martha said, impatiently. "Apparently my blood rotted in the airport. The hospital screwed up."

"I don't believe it. Not after all the trouble you went to. And Neddy cares so much about having your blood."

"Yeah. He was really upset. So am I. I filled out all those forms, mailed them overnight express to Neddy's doctor, donated the blood at the blood bank. The blood was flown to New York. And the stupid hospital couldn't manage to get someone to pick it up at the airport before it rotted."

"How did you find out?"

"They called Neddy."

"Oh, no," I moaned. "They really shouldn't have called him. He must have felt *awful!*"

"Well, they had to call since it was charged to his insurance."

"I'm so sorry, Marth. I know you wanted to be part of the operation."

"Yeah. I did. Enough people have donated blood so that it won't matter, but it still bothers me."

"The whole operation is getting to me. I could hardly sleep the last few nights."

"Are you okay?" Martha liked to take care of me, that was her role as a child. I played into it.

"Oh, Martha. I'm so scared."

"That's normal. Of course you're scared. Remember to breathe every now and then. I hope you get some rest soon." Martha was twenty-six. She'd been acting like an adult since she was four . . .

Neddy had already been admitted when I got to the hospital on the afternoon of Sunday, June 7, 1987. He was still dressed in his own clothes and sat in a chair in his room, talking to an intern. He looked very macho with his arms crossed and sitting up very straight. He waved me into the room.

"Hi, Mom. Sit down," he said. "We'll be through in a second." I limped to a chair and sat down, propping the cane I'd been using for a few months against the wall. My hip operation had been postponed, but I had to keep weight off the joint.

"I'm twenty-four," Neddy said, turning back to the intern, "and still a student. Sometimes it seems like I'll never get through school. Dyslexia. Anyway, I'm in perfect health, except for my heart. Ha. Ha. But you have all the information."

"Thanks," said the intern. He described the procedure that would take place in the morning. First Neddy would get a shot of novocaine. Then a catheter would be inserted into a vein through an incision in his groin. The catheter would be pushed up into his heart, where it would take some pressure measurements. Then dye would be infused through the catheter, and two pictures shot. He'd feel a violent flush when the dye went in for about fifteen to twenty seconds. The pictures would show how much his heart valve was leaking, and how well his heart was pumping.

"Will it hurt when the catheter goes in?" Neddy asked.

"Probably the most discomfort you'll experience will be the prick of the novocaine needle," said the intern. "You won't feel the catheter in your heart at all. But you will feel the flush."

"Are the pictures taken from inside my heart?" Neddy asked.

"No, from the outside. We use two cameras, one above and one below you."

"Oh, I thought it might be a fiber-optic catheter," Neddy joked. He knew about technology, at least a lot more than I did.

"Ha. No, we're not that advanced," the intern said, smiling, easing toward the door.

"Well," I said, when we were alone. "It sounds like everything's under control. Ouch," I added, shifting my weight painfully. The pain from my hip came in spasms.

"Yup," Neddy said politely.

"Bill is taking the day off on Wednesday," I added.

"Good."

"Well, he wanted to. We'll both be here all day."

"How do you like this bed?" Neddy asked, proudly. He was occupying a special electric bed. "I own stock in this company," he said. "Dad had them move this bed in."

"Oh."

"After Wednesday morning," Neddy added, changing the subject, "it's 'Adiós' for two days." He was referring to the expected effects of the anesthesia.

Bill arrived and we went downstairs to the room directly under Neddy's to visit Bill's eighty-seven-year-old mother, Marie Louise, who was having a pacemaker inserted. She was complaining of a draft coming in through the window, which Bill fixed by pushing up the sash with my cane. Marie Louise looked small but surprisingly sturdy.

"Grandmère," Bill asked, "have you had supper?"

"No," she answered, in her French accent, "it has not arrived. But I am not so hungry. My stomach hurts because of all the antibiotic pills." She paused, then pronounced, firmly, "I'm your *mère,* not your *grandmère!*"

We went back upstairs. "You'd better go now. Dad'll be coming in a few minutes," muttered Neddy, nervously. He and Martha were both worried that their father and I would run into each other in the hospital.

The next day when I arrived, Neddy was drugged after the catheterization, having had Valium. He lay with his leg stretched out straight so the incision in his groin wouldn't open. He had to stay that way for eight hours. A pulse in his neck was visibly pounding. His adorably squashed-down Topsiders nestled under the bed table. Someone had given him a little stuffed panda, which sat on the bedside table, along with an orange, apples, a pear, bananas, Poland Spring Water. I had brought him peas in the pod—reminders of the Peapod Store—and strawberries, M & Ms. Neddy's fingernails were ragged and bitten. He wore a plastic identification bracelet around his wrist. The bed visibly jounced from his heartbeat.

As the day passed, his macho demeanor fell away. He asked me to tie his johnnie gown in the back. He asked me to empty the urinal. He wanted me to read Sherlock Holmes out loud.

"Are you a devotee of Sherlock's?" I asked.

"Martha gave me this collection, and I read it sometimes," Neddy answered.

After I read to him, we sat silently. "I cried like a baby during the catheterization," Neddy confided, softly. "The incision didn't actually hurt that much. It was the tension. I just closed my eyes and leaned my head back, and the tears poured."

The night before the operation, Bill was in the kitchen when I got home from the hospital.

"Hi, I'm just cooking some spaghetti for us," Bill said, "and steamed broccoli. Your timing's just perfect. How's Neddy? How are you?" Bill brushed back his gray hair, adjusted his eyeglasses. He looked tired from his long commute. He wore blue jeans with red suspenders holding them up, a plaid shirt, and running shoes. He smiled at me.

"He's a little doped up, but O.K.," I replied. "And me? I need a hug."

We stood in the kitchen hugging each other. "It's going to be all right, little Edith," Bill crooned.

On the day of the operation my anxiety was high but under control. I was rising to the occasion. Arriving at the hospital at 5:30 A.M., I sat in a chair near Neddy's head. He was groggy from a shot.

"They're coming to get me at six," he said, dreamily. "Oh, hi," he added, looking over my shoulder.

His father came into the room and put his briefcase on the hospital dresser. "Hi," Ned answered. He walked over to Neddy's bed, leaned down, and kissed him. "How are you?" he asked, then turned to me and smiled. "Hi," he said.

"I'll get out of here and leave you two alone," I offered, nervously, reaching for my cane.

"That's all right," Ned said.

We sat silently on either side of Neddy's bed, as we had when he had chicken pox, or an earache, when he was a little boy.

About twenty minutes later, Neddy said, "This is the 'I Don't Care Medicine.'"

An orderly wheeled in a narrow stretcher bed, and Neddy eased himself over onto it. He said to Ned, "Give me a kiss." Ned kissed him on the cheek. Feeling a little left out, I came around the bed, leaned over the stretcher, and kissed him, too. I said, "Don't worry."

Ned said, in a jocular way, "The only thing I'm worried about is the stock market."

Neddy, looking very small under his white sheet, was rolled away down the hall. I followed part of the way calling, "I love you. I'll see you later."

In the ICU, Neddy lay flat. His face was deformed, pulled to the side by pink tape which held the blue plastic breathing tube in his mouth. His chest was painted up to his chin with iodine-colored solution. His eyes, rolled up in his head, were slightly open. He looked dead, but his chest rose and fell as the machine breathed him. Four sets of squiggly lines marched past on the monitor.

On my way into the ICU, I had met the cardiologist, Dr. G. He told me that Neddy had arrhythmia—irregular heartbeat caused by inflammation in the heart from the operation.

Neddy's color was ghostly gray, a natural result of anesthesia. The nurse adjusted the rubber tube which carried bloody material from inside his chest to a bag on the side of the bed.

Dr. G had said that Neddy had two kinds of irregular rhythm. The second kind was more dangerous. They were giving him medicine to "head it off at the pass."

Neddy was waking up. I whispered a prayer, then approached the bed gingerly, scared, and took his pale hand. He grabbed mine eagerly. I said, "Neddy, it's Mummy. It's ten of five on the day of your operation, and you're fine. It's all over and you're fine!" He nodded his head.

The nurse asked, "Can you squeeze your mom's hand?" He squeezed my hand hard. "Can you wiggle your toes?" He wiggled them vigorously. His right hand rose up, with tubes dangling, and pointed to his left wrist. "What time is it?" I guessed that he wanted to know. He nodded. "Five of five on the day of your operation." He nodded. Sunlight from a window near the bed shone on his greasy-looking eyelids. The nurse pulled the window shade down and directed the flow of air from the air conditioner away from him.

Neddy drifted off again. I held his hand for fifty minutes while sitting on a plastic trash can, for lack of a chair. My hip throbbed and ached in the unnatural position.

When Bill parted the curtains around the bed and stared in at the scene with a horrified expression on his face, I realized that I had gotten used to what Neddy looked like. Bill studied the still form and me holding the pale hand. He approached, reached around my head and put the tip of his finger in my ear, then took it out and pulled my earlobe. I threw my free arm around his waist and leaned my head against his chest. He put his arm around my shoulders and squeezed, tight.

After Bill had gone back to the waiting room, Neddy woke up again. He wrote on my hand with his finger, "D, A."

"Daddy?" I asked. "Where's Daddy?"

He nodded. "He'll be here soon," I said. "He's at the office."

Neddy's right hand was in a splint that contained most of the tubes leading into his arm. When I gathered up his left hand again, he stabbed awkwardly at his left cheek with the splint. He seemed to be signaling that he wanted a kiss. Tears sprang to my eyes. I leaned over the metal bedside to kiss his cheek, but I couldn't reach him because I didn't dare disturb the tubes leading over the bed rail. "I can't reach you," I murmured, then kissed my fingers and pressed them to his cheek.

The next morning when I arrived at 6:30 A.M., Neddy's breathing tube was out. He wore an oxygen mask which leaked white steam. Later the mask was replaced with a tube leading into one of his nostrils.

Now we held hands constantly. I sat facing the head of the bed and the monitors. Neddy's heartbeat was 113 beats a minute one day, ninety-four the next. The irregular heartbeat was beginning to quiet down. Neddy talked in a hoarse voice. "What is this, Shea Stadium?" he croaked, humorously, when an intern and orderly carried on a loud conversation at the foot of the bed. He said he had only slept about ten minutes at a stretch all night because the tube down his throat made him feel like he couldn't breathe.

The next day, when I got to the ICU, Neddy was in the middle of a workout.

"Hey! Is this your mom?" said a technician who was holding a plastic tube with a mouthpiece to his lips.

"Yes. Hi," Neddy croaked.

"His throat is sore, Mom. He'll be able to speak better soon. Suck in again. I know it hurts, but try to get that ball up the tube."

Neddy sucked on the tube. A ball inside it was lifted an inch or so by his breath. "Oh, come on, you can do better than that," the technician cajoled. "Try to get it all the way up to the top."

Neddy sucked again, and the ball rose a little higher. "Got to get those lungs working," urged the technician. "You're doin' good, Ned. Now I'm going to clap your back. That's to dislodge any mucus that might block your windpipe or bronchioles. Also, we don't want you to get adhesions."

Later, I sat by Neddy's bed and read. He slept with his hand in mine.

I had lunch with my friend Faith in the cafeteria. Faith was going to be admitted into the hospital the next morning. Why did everything happen at once? Her lumpectomy was scheduled for Monday. She was very scared. We held hands and she cried. I felt that if I started weeping, I'd never stop. I couldn't even contemplate losing her.

She said, "My lump feels like a friend."

"Maybe it's a friend you don't need right now."

I got to the cardiac ICU just before they moved Neddy out of intensive care, and walked next to his bed as it was pushed through the halls. Oddly, we ended up in Marie Louise's old room; she had checked out the night before.

The special bed had disappeared; now he lay in a bed with a hand crank.

After the nurse left, Neddy got up and walked to the bathroom to pee. Then he called Ned and asked him to bring some gym shorts. Then he phoned Martha in California and told her about the operation.

After he hung up, he was very tired. He lay speechless for the rest of the day while I sat reading in a corner, but when Ned came, towards the evening, Neddy actually leaped out of bed. He said, quite harshly, to me, "Can you please leave the room while I talk to my father?"

Neddy's heart started to beat irregularly about midnight, and they moved him back to the ICU. When I arrived, he was sitting up looking healthy and pink, but he said he was scared, and added that mental attitude was the key. He had almost lapsed into a depression but had fought his way out of it. Then he talked about a nightmare.

"Listen to this. I had a dream last night. I was in an airplane and almost everyone else had gotten off. There was a man there. I went to the back of the plane to get something. On my way back to the front of the plane, a strong wind was blowing, and the man said, 'We can't get off! We're going to die!' I knew the plane would collapse and explode. I woke up. My heart was pounding. I was terrified. A nurse came in and reassured me that I was O.K."

"Oh, that sounds very frightening," I said, sympathetically.

"I'm often scared, when I wake up in a sweat, for instance, that I'm getting sick and am going to die."

"You know, Neddy, I have dreams that I'm drinking sometimes. They're terribly scary, but I consider dreams like that very healthy. You see, your subconscious is working out your fears. A dream doesn't prophesy anything."

He talked of athletes who have been tested or, worse, haven't been, like pitchers who never made errors in high school and never had to struggle out of adversity.

He talked about my being sober. "I'd wear a sign around my neck, I'd be so proud."

After a couple of days of observation, Neddy was returned to a private room, but he still had to wear a halter monitor, a box that hung from a strap around his neck and recorded the signals from eight electrodes stuck to his chest. He hated being hooked up again, especially since all the needles had been taken out of his veins and the tubes discontinued.

Were the irregular heartbeats an aberration or not? That was what the doctors had to find out.

Neddy was like a time bomb. Everyone was waiting for him to go off.

Bill and I were stressed out. We had both been at the hospital every day, which meant another long subway trip for Bill on top of his commute. Not surprisingly, we were squabbling.

Faith's lumpectomy was over and she was in pain. Cancer had been found in some of her lymph nodes. It would take ten days to find out if the cancer had spread throughout her body. She already knew that she would have to have radiation five days a week for five weeks and then chemotherapy.

I was becoming fixated with Neddy's aftercare. "All I need, Neddy," I told him, "is to hear from the doctor, that's from the doctor, not from you, that it's O.K. for you to stay in that separate area at your father's apartment where no one can hear you."

"Dr. G doesn't deal with parents, children, aunts, uncles, sisters, etcetera, just the patient," Neddy snapped. He added, "You can just put up with the anxiety about this. *I* put up with anxiety, after all. You can't have dyslexia, heart trouble, a perfectionist father, a mother who worries, and NOT have anxiety!"

"You don't have to be rude. Don't worry. I don't want to control you, or restrict you. I simply want some information."

Suddenly Neddy threw back the covers, got out of bed, and headed for the door of his hospital room. "I'll ask at the nurse's station if Dr. G is around," he declared, over his shoulder, and disappeared out the door.

When he came back, Neddy muttered, tersely, "He's coming. Don't know when. Wait here." He got back in bed.

We waited all through *Hawaii Five-O.* I pretended to read but really couldn't. A nurse came in with a white liquid which Neddy was supposed to drink. His hand shook violently and he couldn't pick up the cup, which made me feel it had not been a good idea to bring the subject up, but I was not really sorry.

Finally Dr. G arrived. Neddy said, "Would you please tell my mother I'm all right? Then you can pack up and go, Mother."

"You talk to me first, Ned, and then we'll bring your mother back in. Mom, would you step outside?"

When Dr. G called me back into the room, Neddy had been crying. Dr. G said, pleasantly, "I hear you're going on a trip."

"Yes, I'm hoping to go to a convention, and that's why I want to feel comfortable about Neddy's living situation if he gets out of the hospital while I'm gone. I assume, of course, that he *is* O.K. if you're talking about releasing him."

Dr. G said, "Yes, he is."

"If he gets out of the hospital before I go to California, he's planning to stay with me, and I wanted to ask if he can travel to Long Island?"

"Yes," Dr. G answered.

"Is it O.K. for him to get angry or should we avoid controversial subjects?"

"No, it's better to get it out rather than to stew."

"Are there any restrictions on his diet?"

"No added salt."

I turned to Neddy. "You're not going to like this," I said.

"Go ahead," he said, grimly.

"I won't be able to hear him at night in my apartment. Does that matter?"

"You mean is he going to stop breathing at night?"

"I guess so."

"We send people home to live alone after this operation."

"Well," I said, finally getting to the point, "he's going to stay at his father's, too. There he'll be in what amounts to a separate apartment where no one can hear him."

"Right," said Neddy, "but there's a phone."

"It's fine," said Dr. G. "It's okay for him to stay alone."

"O.K., Mom, that's it, why don't you leave?" urged Neddy, impatiently. "Oh, if you see Faith's daughter, could you ask her to come down?" he added. Faith's daughter had also had a heart operation, and knew how to handle jittery parents.

Up in her room, Faith said, "Perfect love casteth out fear. Your love for Neddy is all you're really guilty of in this situation."

Faith said she wanted to get rid of the "fluff and the clutter" of her life and be closer to God.

Almost two weeks had passed since the operation. Neddy should have been out of the hospital after ten days but he was still hooked up to the monitor. Day after day crept by, and the tension rose. Why didn't they release him? I arrived on the familiar dingy third floor of the hospital and peeked into Neddy's room. He was alone. I eased into the doorway.

Neddy looked annoyed when he caught sight of me. He was becoming more and more grouchy every day.

"They're still not going to let me out," he announced. "I have to have this stress test."

"What? What do you mean?" I asked.

"Look. If you want any information, ask the doctor," Neddy said, wearily. "Just leave me alone."

My sense of dread was growing.

So was my sense of guilt that I had caused this problem for Neddy. It haunted me that my drinking might have had some effect on him when I was pregnant.

Later, in the hospital chapel, a young Catholic chaplain with whom I'd been having long conversations in the cafeteria about my guilt reached over and held my head with his hand. He leaned his own head against mine and, amazingly, sobbed a single sob. "Please," he whispered. "Please forgive yourself."

My face contorted, but I held back the tears. The chaplain released my head and stood up, looked at me piercingly, and then leaned down to take my arm. We walked, sniffling, out of the chapel to the hospital corridor.

Five minutes later I was back in Neddy's room. He looked exhausted. The sprightly front he had kept up for visitors all afternoon was beginning to flag. He slumped in the bed, regarding me sullenly.

"Uh, how are you, uh, feeling?" I stuttered, thrown off by his gaze. "I've been totally wiped out today," I added.

"Oh, no! Do you want me to feel sorry for you?" Neddy sneered, savagely, sitting up straight. "For you? When I'm the one who had the operation? When I have to wait around here for weeks? I can't stand it. You're such a victim. Why don't you get it through your head that I don't want you around? I'm twenty-four years old, this is my room, and I don't want you here. Do you get the message?"

I walked to the door, couldn't make myself leave, came back to the side of the bed. "Look, Neddy. This is hard on me, too. Can't you see?" I pleaded. I walked to the end of the bed and perched on the edge of a chair, muttering, "I can't go, not now, not like this." Dimly I thought, he mustn't get angry, hurt his heart. He got angry the other day and the squiggles on the monitor went crazy.

Now my own heart was pounding. I wanted us to love each other, the way we had in the days immediately following the operation. It was shocking to have returned to the tension that had divided us before the operation.

"I told you I don't want you here." He ripped open his pajama top to reveal the angry scar that stretched from under his collarbone to above his navel. "You did this, and you know it! You're responsible! Because you're an alcoholic! And you drank and smoked while you were pregnant!"

I took a deep breath, oddly warned by my own fears and the chaplain's words, yet cut to the quick. I didn't hesitate, however. I knew what to say. "I refuse to accept that guilt," I stated, firmly. "Not any longer. Not any longer. I've carried it myself for years." Opening the door, I left the room, which was what Neddy had wanted all along.

*   *   *

The next day, miserable and sad, I paced the hospital corridors. Neddy wouldn't speak to me. I saw Dr. G and scurried after him. "May I talk to you for a minute?" I asked.

"Surely," Dr. G answered, gravely, stopping.

"I understand that you have to test Neddy's heart," I began, tentatively. No point mentioning the latest rift.

"Yes. People think that when the operation is over and the patient's alive that's all there is to heart surgery," Dr. G said. He sighed. "Well, often that's not all there is. Sometimes there are fine-tunings that have to be done, and that's what's going on with your son. But he knows all about it. Ask him to tell you. You really shouldn't be using the doctors as intermediaries."

"Intermediaries? Intermediaries? I don't understand. Neddy doesn't tell me much. He hardly communicates with me," I said. "And he's gotten you to agree not to talk to me, either," I mumbled. My old fear of authority figures was upon me.

"I've told him that he must inform you and he will," the doctor said, gruffly. He jingled the change in the pocket of his pants, then started walking. I followed.

"Can you tell me about the test?" I asked.

Dr. G stopped. He turned to me. His face was serious. "Well, we're going to stress his heart so much that it will either duplicate the anomaly, or, if it doesn't, then we'll know that the anomaly was a one-time thing."

What did "stressing his heart so much" mean? How did they plan to do it? With electricity? With exercise? I didn't dare ask. Dr. G continued. "Your son knows all about it. Ask him."

"I told you, he doesn't tell me anything. I know he's an adult and doesn't have to, but it's not fair." My voice trailed off.

"Well," I added, after a minute of silence, "I'm definitely not going to that convention tomorrow."

"I think you should go. The test will take ten minutes. It's scheduled for tomorrow morning. It's not that big a deal. It's important that Ned knows you're keeping up your regular routine. He's fine. Just fine. And you could always get back quickly if we needed you."

*   *   *

I called Neddy from California. "Oh. It's you," he said, sourly. "I'm right in the middle of lunch."

"How did the test go?"

"Fine, fine. They're letting me out tomorrow. Dad's ordered a limo. I'm gonna stay with him. I'm not going to stay with you."

"Oh, Neddy. You were going to spend a whole week with me. You were going to sleep in Martha's room. Can't you move over for a few days after I get back?"

"My lunch is getting cold. Don't call me. I'll call you," he said, in an icy tone.

When I got back to New York after the convention, I had a therapy session.

"I feel guilty," I complained, "for what I said to Neddy in the hospital . . ."

"What you said to Neddy in the hospital was a triumph," Kristina stated. "Don't you see? It's a very important turning point. You won't accept his guilt trips anymore. He's got to take responsibility for his own life. You won't be a victim. You're letting go of him, helping him to let go of you."

I sighed. "I don't know. Maybe it's true. I probably did do it to him. Drinking and smoking when I was pregnant."

"There's no way of proving that," said Kristina. "Anyway, you were suffering from a deadly disease, alcoholism. Under the circumstances, I think you've done a great job with your children. The trouble is, it's become a habit for them to bash you. You don't have to take it anymore. You have a wonderful relationship with them. It may not be easy, that relationship, but it's real."

"How can you say that? When everything is so crummy?"

"But, you see, you're making progress. You're hanging in, persisting, getting through. It may not feel like you are, but you are. You just don't know how to do it, coming from your alcoholic background. You'd better watch out for the self-pity."

"I know. Poor me. Poor me. Pour me a drink."

"You don't have a lot of experience facing crisis without alcohol, even though you've been sober for a long time," Kristina explained. "At other high stress points, like your father's death and Neddy's birth, you had alcohol to help you through. Your emotions were anesthetized. This has been a rough time. You're grieving your son growing up and moving out, and surgery is one of the biggest things that can happen to a family. You've got to be very gentle with yourself."

I took a deep breath, blew it out. "I'll try."

"It's very healthy, you know, that Neddy can express his feelings to you. He's fighting for his life, in more ways than one. He's recovering from surgery, and he's breaking away from you, when you've been so very close. Who else can he blow up at and know for sure will never go away?"

"Are you still angry with me?" I asked, as Neddy got up to leave. It was a month later, his recuperation was over, and we had finally eaten a meal together.

Suddenly the conversation was real after an evening of politeness, awkwardness, and silence. "Yes," he answered. "What began in the hospital is still going on, and I don't understand it. I need some time to figure it out.

"So . . ." he continued, after a minute, "I want to put some space between us when I get back to school. So . . . maybe we shouldn't see or talk to each other until I graduate in January."

"January?" I asked. "It's only July. I don't know," I added, tentatively. "That just seems too long not to see you or talk to you. I know I can't make you change, I mean I'm powerless over you, but it would make me very upset to be out of touch for that long."

Neddy scratched his head and squirmed in his chair. "Well, maybe I could call you each month," he said, slowly, figuring it out. "But don't leave sixteen messages on my machine or send me millions of notes in my postbox," he warned.

I felt cut. Notes and calls, and not sixteen and millions either, were to let him know I loved him.

"I don't want to feel . . ."

"Smothered?" I asked. He nodded and looked down.

"I feel angry at you, too," I said. "Very angry that you didn't include me in your rehabilitation."

Neddy didn't answer. Then he said, "My anger at you is so big. I don't understand it. I just need time to think things out."

"You know, I never could have had a talk like this with my parents. I've become aware how furious I am with them since I've been in therapy. But I would have been too scared to have a conversation like this."

"Why would you have been scared?"

"Because I'd be terrified that they'd go away."

Neddy snorted. "Go away? That would be playing into my hands. I wanted you to go away."

"Anyway, it would have been impossible for me to have a talk like this with my parents."

"I once said to Daddy," he said wistfully, "why can't you talk to me about something real without drinking wine first? And Daddy said his father could never talk to him on a deep level without drinking a lot of martinis."

"Ummm, yes. Well, I think some of it is generational as well. Your father's and my parents weren't trained to talk about deep stuff." I was grateful that he'd shared the confidence about his father, and I didn't want to ruin the gift by attacking Ned or in any way betraying that I might be negative on the subject.

We left it that Neddy would call on the last day of every month. "I think this conversation is a tribute to the fact that, underneath everything, we really have a good relationship," I averred.

"Yeah," Neddy answered, noncommittally, and got ready to go.

CHAPTER FOURTEEN

Waiting for the traffic light to change on a mild day in April, I absently stepped off the curb. A car whizzed by, almost clipping me. I jumped back on the sidewalk. "Don't have an accident, Sweetheart," said a voice from behind me. The voice belonged to a dignified black woman swathed in a long fur coat. She wore several wool hats and pulled a wire cart full of shopping bags. "You have to love yourself, Sweetheart," she imparted, serenely. "To thine own self be true, Sweetheart. Live and let live, Sweetheart."

At the next corner, I heard loud chirrups and looked up. Sparrows nested in the hollow pipe crossbars on a lamppost, and their calls were amplified by their megaphonelike home. As I watched, a bird carrying straw in its beak flew into the pipe.

When I reached my apartment, I set to work on my painting. First I took the huge piece of paper with my giant sketch on it and laid it facedown on the dining room table. I scrubbed along the lines of the sketch, which I could see through the tracing paper, with a soft pencil. Then I pressed that side of the paper to the stretched canvas, and scrubbed along the opposite side of the lines with the pencil, transferring the drawing to the canvas. I had become fascinated by the colors in a show of Fauve art at the Metropolitan Museum, and was particularly taken by *Fishing Port, Col-*

lioure, by André Derain, so I decided to use the same palette for my painting. I planned to use acrylics as a medium.

I had one more pilgrimage to make before the first anniversary of Neddy's death, to my home town. Neddy was living in the same area when he died.

I grew up in Morristown, New Jersey, and moved away when I married at age twenty-two. My father commuted to Manhattan on the old Lackawanna Railroad to his job as a textile merchant from Morristown or next-door Convent Station.

Neddy attended Drew University in nearby Madison, New Jersey. After graduation, he rented an apartment in a converted carriage house in Convent Station.

The week he died, I went to Neddy's apartment to get some of his things, and hadn't been back to New Jersey since.

When I had visited Neddy at Drew and Convent Station, sometimes we went to the place where I grew up.

My parents had rented a house on an old estate about three miles west of Morristown for thirty-five years. In the past the estate had been much bigger, but by the time we lived there it consisted of about a thousand acres. Once it had been grand, but now the gardens, orchards, carriage houses, barns, stables, garages, and greenhouse were either run-down or falling down. The huge main house at the top of the hill was now a two-family dwelling.

The estate had many aspects. There were deep woods full of foxes and deer and birds and thick undergrowth. There were pastures pocked with woodchuck holes, which looked out on a patchwork of fields and trees in the valley below, and on clear days one could see what was then the tallest building in the world peeking up like a smudged and faded stubby finger from behind a distant ridge. There was a large apple orchard, now untended. There was the spot where George Washington's troops had camped for an icy winter, where buttons and old forks could still be unearthed, if one were really lucky, in the depressions that marked the floors of the now-vanished huts. Far down the side of the hill was a swimming pool, fed by icy streams and shaded by evergreen trees.

Linking every aspect of the estate was a serpentine driveway. Washboard rough, it was full of hairpin turns and switchbacks. In winter, it was almost impassable. My parents became experts with tire chains and carried ashes in their cars to throw on icy patches.

Our wooden house stood about halfway up the hill. It was painted white and had black shutters, a gray roof, and a dark green front door. It stood alone, guarded by huge locust trees. A screened-in porch ran along the front of the house, and its brick stoop was ringed by fragrant-smelling boxwood bushes. My favorite climbing tree, a large, luxuriant hemlock, grew near the house.

My father's formal flower garden, which he had built himself, hacking a place for a sloping lawn and flower beds out of a wilderness of arborvitae trees, lay directly below the house. My father often sat on the lawn or on the lip of a flower bed pulling a claw fork through the dirt around the true Solomon's seal, or, laying the fork aside, tying back a rosebush. He was almost always shirtless, and his broad back was tanned nut brown by the sun. He usually wore a pair of long khaki shorts and blue sneakers with white trim, no socks. He kept a large red and white calico handkerchief tucked into his leather belt, for wiping off perspiration. Often his pipe was clenched between his teeth, and tendrils of smoke periodically wreathed his head. A milk bottle, its glass beaded with moisture, leaned in the shade against the base of the locust tree. The bottle was full of cool, clear drinking water. A red wooden wheelbarrow, with one of its sides removed, was often parked on the slope of the lawn.

Later my father might get dressed in his beekeeping clothes: long white trousers, a long-sleeved white jacket with a high neck, gloves, high socks, boots, and a broad-brimmed hat to which netting was attached that completely covered his face. Then he would lift the top off one of the square, white beehives resting on table-like stands near the garden. A cloud of agitated bees soon swarmed up and surrounded him. He'd pump smoke at the buzzing insects from a bellows contraption he held in his hand. Then he'd lift frames full of waxy dark honeycomb out of their slots, and insert empty frames. Later we'd eat the dark honey, rich with nectar from locust blossoms, with butter on fresh cornbread baked in the shape of corncobs in the iron mold in the kitchen.

A large horse chestnut tree loomed over the south side of the house. My wooden swing hung from its branches. At the back of the house was a tangled jungle of brambles, honeysuckle, small trees, and my sister Nancy's "grave."

Nancy's grave had been dug by our brothers to torture her,

because she was terrified of death. The grave was most perfectly visible through the bathroom window as you sat on the toilet, which is how my brothers planned it. "See?" Phil and Ken would call, banging on the bathroom door. "See? Take a good look. There's your grave, fresh and open, ready and waiting."

The bathroom door would wrench open violently, and Nancy would run out. "They're horrid! And awful! Can't you stop them, Mummy?" she would beg. "Dad, help me. Don't you see how mean they are?" Our parents were sympathetic, but the grave stayed there, a rectangular four-foot-deep hole with a pile of dirt next to it. Gradually, over the years, it filled in with leaves and the sides caved in.

The house was smaller than one would expect for a family of six and two live-in servants. There were four rooms downstairs, a library where my father had his desk, the living room, the dining room, and kitchen/pantry. Upstairs were two bathrooms, the master bedroom, the boys' room, and Nancy's room. At the back of the house on the second floor were two tiny rooms for my nurse, Yoyo, and me.

The attic, a place of mystery and old clothes, housed a bedroom for Sophronia, our cook, when she was there, depending on whether times were fat or lean, as well as storage space. The cellar, less mysterious than the attic but susceptible to ominous dribbles of water from outside, held firewood, old *National Geographic*s, home-canned vegetables and jellies, and a bin full of shiny black coal for the furnace and the stove.

Before I was born and when I was a baby, we owned a pointer named Hundred, Hundie for short, who lived outside under the porch or in the cellar. His name came from the numerous brown spots on his hide. When I was about four, Hundred died and we acquired a golden retriever named Swithin.

My bedroom was truly small, and almost completely filled with furniture. There was just enough space for a bureau and, right next to it, a small desk, which was often cluttered with schoolbooks when I got old enough to go to school. Above the desk was a window that looked into my parents' bathroom. My room had been added on to the house and was built over an existing window. A dark green shade covered the glass panes. Next to the desk was a narrow bookcase. My football helmet, a pile of comic books, my plastic Tom Mix Ralston Straight Shooter Signal Arrowhead with built-in compass and whistle, and my radio were lined up on top of the bookcase. Another window at the end of the tiny room looked out at the horse chestnut tree and my swing. A standing lamp with an attached shelf was my bedside table, next to my wooden bed, which was painted blue. The bed was jammed snug up to the walls at its head, side, and foot. On the wall next to the bed hung a large canvas map of the United States.

The day started when my father carried a bucket of coal up the cellar steps, took an iron spike, pushed it into a hole in our two-burner coal stove, and rattled it around in the hole. That made a lot of gray and glowing ashes fall down inside the stove. He opened a door in the stove and shoveled the hot ashes out into a pail. Then he removed the caps on the burners and poured shiny, black new lumps of coal into the openings. The stove had a top oven—very hot, for cooking—and a bottom oven for warming plates. A twist of the spigot that stuck out of its front released boiling water.

After my beloved Yoyo, a tiny (4'11") British woman with crimped gray hair, dark quizzical eyebrows, gnarled arthritic hands, and a mischievous monkey face, left because we couldn't afford to have her work for us any more, my mother braided my hair every morning. My brown hair was so long that I could sit on it if I leaned my head back. Now it crackled with static electricity. My mother switched from the brush to a comb to unknot a tangle. "Ouch!" I yelped.

The thick tooth at the end of the comb drew a part straight back from the middle of my forehead, and my hair was divided into two sections. My mother's strong fingers then divided one of the sections into three equal parts, and began to interweave them. "Ouch!" I exclaimed again. The first few plaits were woven tight against my scalp, pulling the tender hairs painfully, but after that the braiding was painless and went swiftly, until I heard the twang of a rubber band as it was wrapped around and around my braid, about an inch from the end. Soon the second braid was done.

If there was time before school, I liked to look at the top of my mother's bureau. Near the front, there was a picture frame with a picture of my mother's parents, Granny and Gampy, in it. Next to the picture frame was a buttonhook with a yellowing ivory handle and a matching hairbrush with soft bristles. Behind them was a round, silk-lined box from my mother's trip around the world. Inside was a necklace made of amber, my mother's favorite jewelry. The honey-colored blobs glowed up at me. I lifted the necklace and pressed it to my cheek. I liked to feel the amber when my mother unfastened it from her neck and it was still warm. Now it was cool. At the back of the bureau were some Chinese shoes on stilts. A painted American Indian pot was next to the shoes, and a couple of blue-and-white spiraled marbles from my mother's marble collection. An old doll with a corncob body rested against the pot, its legs askew.

"Dithie! Time to go. Hurry up!" came my mother's voice from downstairs. "Dad's going to miss his train!"

Years before, when I was a baby, my father danced with me every morning before he left for his train. It was part of the ritual. When breakfast was over, the rest of the family crowded into the living room for the dance, sitting on the black horsehair sofa or the chintz-covered armchair or the straight-backed chair near the telephone table. My father, freshly shaved and smelling of Aqua Velva, with a yellow rose in the lapel buttonhole of his gabardine suit, picked me up, held me to his chest with one arm, and grasped my right hand in his in a dance position. "Ta tata tata, tata, tata," he sang, and waltzed me around in circles, dipping and swaying until I giggled, happily, my head thrown back. In my memory, the sun was always shining, making a rainbow on the rug where it came through the window and refracted through the prisms on the windowsill. My father never missed that dance, even if he was late for the train. Some mornings he just had to take the 7:41 instead of the 7:23.

Now that I was older, my father drove me to school on his way to his train. Later in the afternoon, my mother picked me up, and we drove together around the town to do errands. We went to the cleaners, to the laundry, to the grocery store. We picked up an angel food cake at the bakery.

My mother was always rushing. She was always tapping her thumb on the steering wheel. Her impatient frown had become engraved on her face. She coughed more when she was nervous.

Finally, we drove to "the Hollow," a low-lying part of town. The houses got shabbier and shabbier the farther down into this section we descended. Going there was worth it, though, as far as my mother was concerned, because her favorite secondhand bookstore was in the Hollow. My mother stopped the car in front of a ramshackle shop with jerry-built tables of books outside. We parked and got out of the car. "What have you got today, Mr. Turturro?" my mother would inquire of the bent old man who stood in the door of the shop. He wore a large cardigan sweater around his thin shoulders. Secretly, I didn't like him much. He had a strange, raspy voice, and he spat when he talked.

Mr. Turturro was smart. He knew a thing or two about books. But so did my mother. They played the game of trying to trick each other out of gems from someone's estate. "This batch came in today," Mr. Turturro would rasp, casually turning away. "Look 'em over."

My mother would leaf quickly through the books, studying copyright dates and quality of engravings and whether there was mildew on the pages. She liked old books about dead people and people who thought they could talk to them, prisons, circus freaks, soldiers, old toys, railroads, animals, children, assassinations. Swiftly she'd make her decision, gather up an armload of books, and take them to Mr. Turturro.

"Four dolla," Mr. Turturro would say, scratching his arm under his cardigan sleeve with long, dirty fingernails and spraying a fine mist of spit as he spoke.

"What? These old things? You know you were going to throw them away. All of them together are worth two dollars, at most. The only interesting one is this children's book, and it's worth a quarter," my mother would counter.

"You've got seven there. Three-fifty. Last offer."

"All right, but it's a crime."

My mother read every volume. White pieces of paper bristled out of each one, marking interesting passages. Gradually, over the years, her books filled our house. First bookcases of every shape and size were crowded into my parents' bedroom. Then came the books which filled every bookcase and teetered in piles on top of them. Bookcases spread out into the upstairs hall landing, into the back hall, the attic, even the cellar. When there was no more space for bookcases, piles of books grew under the beds and behind doors. Books finally covered my father's bed entirely, and he had to sleep in the boys' room when they were away at school. My mother got a storeroom downtown, but that didn't seem to lessen the crowding.

Every book was important, because my mother was a scholar, and she had to do research. She did it by reading, but also by going. She went to the Midwest and climbed down into a workmen's ditch to find out what mud was like a hundred years ago. She looked through an old camera, peed in an ancient commode, lit up oil lamps to test the quality of their light. She visited a barber's school to watch the student barbers shave inflated balloons, and rode on a garbage truck to find out what collecting garbage was like. She was constantly looking up facts. Did baby elephants ever fall into their parents' footsteps? (They did.) Did whale calves ever get jellyfish stuck in their throats? (Sometimes.) Did gorillas sleep in nests up in trees? (Almost always.)

By the time I was six or seven years old, my brothers and sister were away at school, so I spent a lot of time alone. One of my favorite places was high up in my climbing tree next to the house. I found a place where two branches crossed, forming a comfortable seat, and spent hours there, hidden among the branches, watching the green needles dance in the breeze, eating Mallomars and reading books about Joan of Arc, which I hauled up by rope.

If I wasn't up in the tree, I was playing in the woods. I made a "thinking hole," in the manner of my hero, Freddy the Pig, the subject of twenty-six books by Walter R. Brooks. Once Freddy had dug a hole to trap someone, and the trap proved singularly ineffective, so he put a mattress in the bottom of it and used it for thinking. I liked the concept, and made my own "thinking hole" in the center of a forsythia bush. There was no mattress, and no hole, just a little clearing in which to be concealed, and to dream.

At other times, I played with a friend named Muffie, who also lived on the hill, and her little brother. Once, in a particularly snowy winter, we built an igloo, and we spent long afternoons sliding on kitchen trays down icy, steep pastures. At other times, usually in the long, sweltering summers, when my mother wrapped handkerchiefs around her wrists to keep the sweat from running onto what she was writing, my playmates and I were often stricken with boredom and didn't know what to do with ourselves. Then we'd "play a story," which meant that each of us would suggest three scenarios, and then we'd vote and choose which one to act out. Circus, for instance, meant swinging on the rings on a gymnasium set. Robin Hood meant climbing on the Greenwood Tree, a gigantic pine whose lower branches grew almost vertically and were a perfect hiding place for Robin Hood's Merry Men. Camping meant pretending to camp out in the woods in small huts we had built out of bark. That one was lots of fun because I got to use my army surplus mess kit and my canteen, and my jackknife, from which folded out a can opener, a corkscrew, a minute pair of scissors, a spike for piercing things, and two knife blades. Pirates meant playing beneath another great tree that stood like a mast in a prow-shaped cleft in the unpaved road near the apple orchard. Rodeo meant riding sticks, quirting ourselves on the flank as we galloped and then roping and throwing steers and taming bucking broncos. Indians meant sliding behind trees with silent toe-heel tread and taking scalps from unsuspecting victims. Tarzan meant swinging from thick, ropy grapevines that grew on trees in back of my house. Exploring meant venturing into unfamiliar territory at the back of the hill, where there were mysterious ponds and deep vegetation, with snakes and frogs and unknown things.

We had costumes to go with every story: chaps with fringes, vests, tights, green flannel jackets, feathered headdresses, capes made of towels which we knotted around our necks.

Thirty years later, I went back with Neddy.

"The underbrush is dying off. Remember what a jungle it used to be?" asked Muffie, who lived in the same house she'd lived in when we played together so long ago. We were standing on the lawn. She gestured towards the surrounding woods. "No one can figure it out, whether it's the deer eating everything or acid rain. There's no underbrush in the woods anymore."

"This is damage caused by deer," she continued, pointing at a dogwood which lacked flowers on its lower limbs.

"I want to climb my old tree," I said, changing the subject. I was anticipating seeing my climbing tree and the old white house. Muffie had obtained the present owners' permission for us to visit.

"I think they've pruned all the trees around your house," Muffie remarked. "But you'll see. They're expecting you."

Neddy and I walked down the hill, shrunken now by time, to my old house. The owner's wife, Kate, was gardening in a flower bed near my father's old beekeeping shop.

"Hello. Are you Kate? I'm Edith," I said, holding out my hand.

"Hello. I'm glad to meet you," said Kate, standing up and removing her gardening glove so she could shake my hand.

"And this is Neddy," I said. Neddy and Kate shook hands.

"Nice to meet you," he said politely, with a grin.

"There's my tree," I said, pointing to the big hemlock next to the house. I had been telling Neddy about the Mallomars and the books and the lush needles that completely hid me. "Uh-oh, it doesn't look very healthy."

"That tree? It's sick. It's coming down soon," said Kate. We walked close to the big hemlock. All its branches were trimmed off for about twenty feet up the trunk. The remaining branches were almost bare and their sparse needles gray and brittle, withered. "It's a hemlock. All the hemlocks are dying. They're infected by the woolly adelgid, an insect that removes sap and injects a toxic spittle," Kate continued.

"How awful," I moaned. "How awful. What's happening to the world?" I gazed up the trunk. "I wish I could climb it. I had a seat, way up there, where two branches crossed. I was completely hidden by the thick needles. It was a secret place. I used to sit up there for hours."

"Well, you can go in the house if you like," said Kate after a minute of silence. "Just ignore the mess."

"Thank you. We'd love to. By the way, what are you making over there?" My father's sloping lawn and the flower beds were gone. The land had been flattened out, leaving a large, muddy expanse. A bulldozer was parked under a tree.

"Don't ask. I don't," said Kate, scratching her head. Her expression was mock-exasperated. "My husband started that a year ago when he filled in the old holding tank. I don't know what it's going to end up as."

The area around the house was beautifully landscaped, the jungle behind it gone. Lawn and neat evergreen seedlings covered the area where Nancy's grave used to be.

"We'd love to go in for a minute, if you're sure that's all right," I said.

"Sure," said Kate, kneeling and beginning to transplant a petunia from a box. "Go ahead. Just ignore the mess."

The wooden front door was just the way I remembered it; the same ornate brass knocker, the same dark green paint. Neddy and I stepped into the front hall. We paused to look up at the staircase and heavy wooden banister. Then I grabbed Neddy's arm and drew him into the dining room, to our left. I narrated as we made a circuit of the ground floor. "This was the dining room. Uh, those light fixtures are the same, just the same, but all of this furniture, of course, wasn't there. We used to eat here every night. This area was the pantry where Dad kept his plants. He had a green thumb. His plants grew like crazy. There's no wall here, there used to be a wall here. Oh, look, they've remodeled the kitchen and made it into a family room, extended it out where the back porch used to be. Now they watch TV here. It's nice. The coal stove is gone. They use gas. This used to be a pantry back here where we stored canned food, now it's the laundry room. Gee, you can walk right into the library from here. There used to be a wall here, too. This is where Granddaddy's desk used to be. It looks pretty much the same in here, except smaller. The whole house is so small. This is the living room. Dad used to dance with me every day in here before he caught his train. You've heard that story. Look at this Victorian furniture, it goes with the house."

"Cool. It's really neat. Shall we go up?" Neddy asked. We were standing in the front hall again, having completed our circuit. Neddy was a little impatient, but truly interested. He was usually interested in family history.

"Sure. Do you think we dare?" It seemed like an invasion of privacy to visit the bedrooms upstairs.

"Yeah. She said it was O.K."

"All right, just for a minute."

We climbed the stairs and headed for the back of the house. Yoyo's room was now a study, barely big enough to hold a desk, lamp, and filing cabinet.

"Wow. Did you really sleep in here?" Neddy asked.

"No. Yoyo slept in here. I slept in this one," I said, entering the next room. The wall and window between my bedroom and my parents' bathroom had been removed, and my bedroom had be-

". . . the same dark green paint."

come a walk-in closet, filled with suits and dresses. The walls were lined with shoes on racks.

"Can you believe I actually fit in here?" I marveled, leaning into the spotless closet.

"It doesn't seem big enough for a bed."

My parents' bathroom was remodeled but the familiar bathtub with claw feet was still there. The flood of memories became painful, I missed my parents so. I hurried Neddy through the rest of the house. Phil and Ken's room and Nancy's room were nicely fixed up. The bookcases were long gone and light streamed in the windows of my parents' old room. Neddy and I clattered down the front stairs. It hurt to linger too long.

Outside, we stood on the porch. The box bushes in front of the house were gone, replaced by rhododendrons. From the woods came the melancholy cry of mourning doves. Now I couldn't wait to get away.

"Thank you for letting us go in," I said to Kate. "You've done a beautiful job."

"You're welcome. Come again anytime."

*   *   *

Now, preparing for my trip to New Jersey in April 1991, I packed a plastic bag stuffed with ice cubes and a washcloth, in case I needed to bathe my eyes. I imagined I might cry so hard that I would veer off the road.

When I arrived at Convent Station, I parked in someone's driveway across the street from Neddy's carriage house apartment and mopped my tears with the washcloth. Later I drove past the bank where Neddy had worked, the hotel where he had been night clerk, and the post office where he had gotten his mail.

Then I traveled out the old highway and turned up the familiar winding driveway, still washboard rough. Negotiating the switch-backs and hairpin turns, I passed the Greenwood Tree, and kept climbing until I reached the apple orchard, parking under the "pirate ship's" tall masts, where I used to practice smoking when I first learned to drive.

This part of the old estate had been absorbed by a park, and was now federal land. That, and the fact that the hill was steep, had kept it from being developed for real estate.

A cluster of twenty or so deer watched me as I got out of the car. They moved into the woods when I started to climb the hill, passing decayed stumps of apple trees. Deer had multiplied in this area so much that they had become a major nuisance, devouring homeowners' gardens and shrubbery and damaging the forest.

Near the top of the hill, I came upon an area about twenty feet square with a wire fence around it. A sign announced that this was a DEER EXCLOSURE, fenced off to give underbrush a chance to grow so scientists could assess the extent of damage attributable to animals, as opposed to acid rain. The undergrowth inside the wire fence was luxuriant, but outside and under the trees in the nearby woods, there was sparse vegetation.

The gigantic pines at the top of the hill were dead, their serrated trunks silhouetted against the sky. I looked out toward the horizon where I used to view the stubby finger of the Empire State Building, but a new growth of trees hid the vista.

As I began to descend the other side of the hill, an incessant roaring penetrated my ears. The noise was traffic passing on a superhighway in the once-silent valley below.

A tiny graveyard lay in a grove of smaller, living pines. I entered the graveyard through a wooden arch around which were entwined thick, ropy grapevines. A few gravestones marked the burial places of the family who had once owned the estate.

I thought of the white-haired Quaker matriarch and patriarch of that family, so gentle and soft-spoken, and how they used to give me a prickly concoction ("Would thee like a drink of ginger ale and grape juice?") on their porch before reading aloud a daily nature story by Thornton Burgess from the newspaper. Bertha would compose herself, cross her wide ankles encased in tan cotton stockings, bend her tightly ringleted head, peer through her thick glasses, and begin to read. After the story, Bertha and her husband would go for a walk with their ancient spaniel, Trixie. Often they were joined by their daughter, who wore Western shirts and soft twill pants and sometimes carried a pistol in a holster at her waist. Later Bertha would retire to a five-foot-tall wooden orgone box with a breathing hole in it. She would take off all her clothes and sit on a chair in the box, to cure her ailments.

I said a few prayers, then descended on an overgrown path to the "Ring Road," which encircled the crown of the hill. My father used to run here before breakfast thirty years ago. Turning left on the dirt road, I passed the stone marker commemorating Stark's Brigade, the part of George Washington's army which had camped on the hillside for that bitterly cold winter more than two centuries ago, and walked back to my car through the bare, silent woods.

Driving down the driveway, I passed the old house. My climbing tree was gone, and smooth green lawn covered the place where it used to stand.

CHAPTER FIFTEEN

In mid-April I visited my sister on the North Shore near Boston, and my brother in Cambridge.

I waved goodbye to Ken, who had wheeled my suitcase into the air terminal, kissed me, and now drove off in his car.

It was at this airport, on Easter Sunday eighteen years ago, that I had asked my sister for help, showing Nancy the beer can in my purse. *See? I have to have it with me all the time. I can't get on this plane without my fix. I can't stop drinking. There's no hope. Absolutely none. And the shrink said, "Your children are in danger. Your children are in danger. You'd better get other help. I can't help you. Your children are in danger."*

Memories of that last weekend of drinking eighteen years ago flooded back.

In the plane's lavatory, I had drunk the beer in a couple of gulps, tipping back my head and opening my throat.

I took a taxi from LaGuardia to my apartment. The bready smell of booze oozed out of my pores. My skin was stretched tight over the bloat like the skin of overripe fruit, ready to split. I knew what I looked like. Stringy long hair. Dead eyes. I carried smelling salts in my pocketbook along with a couple of dirty, lint-covered ten-milligram Valiums.

When I was safely inside my apartment, I went directly to the kitchen before taking off my coat, and got out the ice. Plenty of cubes in a sixteen-ounce glass. Four inches of vodka. V-8. Ahhh. That's better. Must remember to order a new case tomorrow.

Sometime that evening the children returned from spending the weekend with their father. The next day they went to school. After they left, I heaved over the toilet bowl, puking up bile. I called in sick to my job at the department store. *They're getting wise to me. I've had flu too many times. Oh, who cares?*

Shit. I'd forgotten to put the beer in the fridge. It was piss-warm. I shoved three big cans into the freezer, popped open a warm can. The bubbles made me gag. I ran to the kitchen sink, spewed up the liquid, gasped and retched some more, bringing up nothing.

Finally the beer stayed down. I walked to the bedroom, settled down on the bed. The sheets had little round burn holes from my cigarettes. Gotta be careful. "Your children are in danger." It was true. I couldn't bear to lose custody, if it ever came to that. I loved them so much. Also, everyone would know.

I got up and turned on the television. Soon the game shows would come on. They were soothing, and something of a challenge. I liked to call out the answers. I was pretty good at *Jeopardy* and *Password,* although *Jeopardy* verged on being too hard.

I Love Lucy was on. It was the episode where Ricky messed up the apartment. "You can't 'spect me to live in a museum," he said to Lucy. "Ricardo the First, King of the Slobs," Lucy retorted. Lucy decided to pay him back by dividing the apartment in half. His side was the messy side. Her side was the neat side.

I was getting high now. During the commercial, I walked to the kitchen, pulled one of the beers from the freezer. It was just beginning to freeze, the amber liquid turning to spiky geometric slivers, crunchy in the mouth. Ahhhh. This was the way I liked it. Nice and cold. I began to feel happy, normal. I told myself to be sure to get to those other beers before they froze.

I called the liquor store, ordered two quarts of vodka. "Oh, and throw in a bottle of bourbon and a half-gallon jug of Almadén wine. I'm having a party," I explained to the clerk.

Lucy had littered the apartment with laundry and garbage and live chickens, to embarrass Ricky in front of a reporter. She dressed up as a hillbilly, and scratched herself energetically. "I've seen her do strange thins before," said Ricky in his inimitable accent, to Fred Mertz. " 'Splain this if you can."

The key turned in the lock. I got up, put on my wrapper, tried to pull it closed over my big body. Miss Connor came in the front door, put down a package on the hall table, and went to the coat closet to hang up her coat. "Good morning," she said, in her soft Irish accent. "I brought the beer. Did you have a nice Easter?"

"Wonderful. My trip was lovely," I gushed. "Thanks. I'll put it in the icebox. Oh, no!" I exclaimed, running for the freezer. "Hell's bells!" The beer in the two remaining cans was almost solid, barely sloshing when I shook the cans. When Miss Connor went in the children's rooms to make the beds, I popped open a can. Cold foam poured unnaturally out of the pop-top hole. I licked the foam out of the hole. Have to let it set for a while. Or maybe it's time to start the vodka. I took the open beer out the back door, buried it deep in my neighbor's garbage can. I poured myself a vodka and V-8.

In the late afternoon, I woke up lying on the bed with my face resting in my lunch plate. I stumbled to the bathroom, washed the dried specks of cottage cheese off my cheek, and tried to clean my hair. The children and Miss Connor must have gone to the park. The telephone rang. The sound sent a thrill of fear through my body. Who could be calling me? Confusedly, I picked up the receiver.

"Hello?" Muffie's voice asked. "Edith? How are you?"

Sure. Who else could it be? Muffie was the last of my friends to hang in.

"Oh. Fine. Fine," I answered.

"This man has been calling me. Your sister gave him my number. He wants to know if you need help."

"No! No, thanks. I'm just fine. I can't talk to anyone now. Thank you. I have to go," I said. I hung up.

Somehow the evening passed. The children were in bed. I postponed eating so that I could feel the maximum effects of a new infusion of booze. Now I was lurching, weaving. On my way to the bathroom, I stumbled into the television set, slipped and fell, crawled on my hands and knees over the threshold to the bathroom and its blessedly cool tiles, vomited again at the bowl.

So went the next few days. Each morning I woke up sweating, my body drenched, threw up, and gagged down the first few sips of booze. The order from the liquor store was used up, so I drank the disgusting leftover brands that I hated from the back of the liquor cabinet. Tía María. Rum. Crème de menthe. My hand shook so hard I often couldn't get a glass to my lips, so I lowered my face to its rim, and lapped up the contents. I swallowed pills from my hoard to try to cure the shaking, and the fear. Now I heard a baby crying, crying, crying inside my head.

"Tell Uncle Phil I'll be right in," I said to Martha.

"We're not at his house, Mummy," Martha replied, in an angry tone.

"But . . ."

"See?" said Martha, leading me to the window. "There's the street? See?"

"Yes, Mummy. See?" piped Neddy.

Yes. There was the familiar street, with people walking peacefully on the sidewalks. Some of them even held leashes with dogs attached. But the baby was still crying, crying. And your children are in danger.

"There's a man on the telephone," said Miss Connor.

How could I talk on the phone? I was so sick, so very, very sick. *I swear I'll never drink again. Tomorrow, when my hand is steady enough to write legible letters, I'll pen again, "Gave up booze" on my calendar. In ink, because ink makes it true. No. Come to think of it, I'll never write that again. Because I can't promise, even promise myself, anymore.*

"Hello?" I said into the receiver.

"Hello, my name is Newt," the deep voice rumbled, and the healing began.

I hadn't had a drink from that day to this, since I first heard the message of hope that there was a way I could stop drinking. Talk about a miracle. Now I celebrated the eighteenth anniversary of that day.

When the pilgrimage to New Jersey was over, about a month and a half remained before the first anniversary of Neddy's death —which I now began to anticipate with dread—so I forced myself to review the last three years of his life.

By the end of August 1987, two months after his heart operation, Neddy was jogging four miles a day. In September he started school again. He was majoring in computer science with a minor in business management. Computer languages for his major included PASCAL and BASIC. He took two data structure courses and worked on Digital's VAX system and the Epson QX–16 microcomputer. For his minor, he took courses in managerial economics, macro-, microeconomics, and business ethics. Sometimes he studied in the library for eighteen hours at a stretch. He called me on the last days of July, August, and September, and we got together in October; I drove out to Drew and we watched a soccer game together. The crisis between us seemed over, but I was still deeply shaken by his accusation in the hospital. Soon after seeing him, I wrote him a letter.

Dear Neddy,

This is an amends letter.

Of course I regret terribly having smoked and drunk when I was pregnant. At that time, doctors didn't tell people to stop smoking or drinking when they were pregnant.

I have felt guilty for years that something I might have done might have caused you or Martha some physical effects. Perhaps this is true, I don't know, but I can't carry that guilt anymore. I love you very much and I would never knowingly hurt you. But I also feel I have a disease (alcoholism) which in its active stages makes one blind to many things.

I want to point out, too, that you have another parent who has a heart murmur.

I'm sorry that you had to go through what you went through. You were very brave in a tough situation. I know you want to leave that all behind you now.

I'll talk to you soon.

Lots of love, Mummy

He appreciated my letter and wrote back about his plans. Our arrangement to talk only once a month was dissolved at this point.

In December 1987, Neddy finished his academic work at Drew, ending up with a grade point average of 2.76 overall. He decided not to graduate in January 1988 but to wait until June when his class graduated. In the meantime, he pumped gas at a gas station

while interviewing for jobs, and found his apartment in the converted carriage house in Convent Station. I felt relieved that he
was managing his own life so well.

He had emerged from the educational system onto the job market at a time when a profound change was taking place. For generations, college-educated Americans had expected steady employment by one company for their entire working lives, with
promotions and rising incomes until retirement. Each generation
expected to surpass the last in income. Now college graduates
anticipated shorter employment at lower wages, fewer benefits,
and less secure prospects for the long run.

We got together for Christmas. Among other things, Neddy
gave me a pair of earmuffs, and I gave him a Dustbuster for cleaning his new apartment. At Easter, we drove up to a restaurant in
Connecticut.

". . . and I gave him a Dustbuster . . ."

At the end of the meal, Bill asked for the check. His mother,
Marie Louise, turned to me with a wry look on her face. "In
France, it's called *'l'addition,'*" she said. "Or, for a joke, *'la
douloureuse.'*"

I laughed and pushed away my coffee cup.

"Duck, duck, goose," said Neddy, looking out of the window of the restaurant at some ducks on a pond. "Uh-oh," he added, rolling his lower lip out quizzically, just like his father did, and peering even harder at the birds. "Mating time. Wagging the bottom time. Flapping the wings time."

"Thank you," said Bill to the waitress, who had brought the check.

"Un excellent répas," murmured Marie Louise, contentedly.

"Wasn't it nice?" I asked. "I'm so glad I heard about this place. The only complaint I have is the noise."

"Les cries forts."

The low ceiling and the loud voices of the Easter diners in the alcove of the country restaurant had made conversation difficult, but we had managed to discuss Neddy's new job at a bank. He was tremendously relieved to have landed it after pumping gas for three and a half months. We also touched on politics, automobiles, sports, news of Bill's five children, and Martha in California.

"Neddy. Did you like the book?" Marie Louise inquired.

"What?" Neddy inquired, turning away from the window.

"Marie Louise gave you a book when you were in the hospital," I reminded him.

"Oh, I forgot," answered Neddy. "I don't remember a whole lot about the operation. I think I was on really strong drugs. Anyway, I couldn't really read. I just watched TV. Sorry," he added, apologetically. "Hey," he burst out. "Do you know I'm part pig? Oink. Oink. That's why I eat so much. Get it? From the pig valve."

"We didn't have these drinks," Bill said, studying the check. "They've made a mistake. Why don't I get this straightened out and meet you outside?"

Marie Louise, Neddy, and I strolled by the pond. Ducks flew in from upstream and landed with a flurry. "It's cool the way they do that," Neddy said, watching them coast to a stop.

We celebrated Neddy's graduation from college in June. He was twenty-five years old.

Neddy held my graduation present, a glass bear from Steuben, in his hand. He read the printed description of it aloud. " 'To dream of a bear presages happiness. In folklore, the bear is a guardian spirit, standing for strength, bravery, and long life.' Neat!

I love it. Thank you, Mummy. I'll have to find a special place for it in my apartment. Thanks for the gift certificate at Brooks Brothers, too."

Bill and I, Neddy, and Dr. Jansky, who was one of the experts on dyslexia who had helped Neddy over the years, were dining at Windows on the World, the restaurant atop of one of the towers of the World Trade Center. A hazy view of skyscrapers and the distant Central Park loomed in the floor-to-ceiling windows behind us.

"Happy graduation," I replied, grinning. "You've done such a great job. I just love where you are in your life now. You have a wonderful, philosophic outlook."

"Well, when you've been through heart surgery, you kind of stop worrying about the little things."

Dr. Jansky spoke up. "I have a present for you, too, Ned. Do you want to open it now?"

"I sure do." Neddy tore the wrapping paper off a big box. "A juicer! Great! Now I can have fresh orange juice!"

"Or carrot juice. Or beet juice," said Bill.

"Thank you," said Neddy to Dr. Jansky.

"You've had a long haul, and it's been very tough with the dyslexia, but you stuck in there. It's a very great triumph," Dr. Jansky replied. "Congratulations."

Bill handed over two small wrapped packages. "Here's something from me," he said, smiling.

Neddy opened the packages. "Neat! A penknife! And a pen! It's a beauty. Thank you, Bill. Thank you, everybody."

A letter arrived a few days later. Neddy's familiar handwriting scrawled across the page.

Dear Mom

Thanks so much for the graduation party. It was so much nicer with you and Bill and Dr. Jansky than it would have been at school with all those other people.

I am glad you are impressed with where or what I am. It's a positive reflection on you, that through all the ups [the scrawl jumped above the rest of the sentence] and downs [the writing dipped below the rest of the sentence] you have helped mold a strong, brave, and long living son. (Sound familiar? I'll give you a hint; think bear.) Take care! Lots of love!! Neddy.

Over the next year, life remained tranquil. I was relieved not to be so involved with Neddy or going through a crisis. Every once in a while, I traveled out to Convent Station to visit him, or he came to see me in the city. One time he gave me a present of a T-shirt with the message, INSANITY IS HEREDITARY—YOU GET IT FROM YOUR KIDS. Another time he was very excited because he had bought a car, a red Toyota Starlet. He loved driving fast, and bought a CB radio. He went parasailing. He informed me that he was bicycling twenty-two miles a day without a safety helmet. It almost seemed that he had to push my buttons every once in a while by imparting this kind of information. I called him a fool.

"He went parasailing."

On one of the visits, we had a long talk about finances, his future, love, marriage.

"How will I *know* when I'm in love?" Neddy asked, wistfully. "Why didn't you ever talk to me about marriage?"

"Because I made a mess of it, that's why. How could I possibly give you advice when I was such a dismal failure at it? By the way, you're so far ahead of where Daddy and I were when we first met. I mean, your whole generation is much more honest and open. You know yourself so much better than we ever did."

At the end of September 1988, when Martha was in New York for a visit, the three of us strolled through Central Park to the zoo. On the way, Martha and Neddy posed for photographs at the Alice in Wonderland statue. Hazy sunlight filtered through the trees. It was a beautiful warm day. Our mood was joyful, easy.

At the zoo, we watched the sea lions being fed. They clapped their flippers, leaped for fish, put on a show. Up in his rocky domain, the polar bear lunged through the water next to the Plexiglass window that gave spectators a view of him underwater as well as on land. The rain forest with its sluggish snakes and the polar ice cap with its active penguins were beautiful. We ate lunch in the outdoor restaurant. Neddy ate only French fries, a Coke, and an ice cream cone, which worried me. I wished he would take better care of himself. We laughed and laughed.

Later, Martha leaned her cropped head on my shoulder as we sat near the Delacorte Clock, waiting for it to chime and for its sculptured animals to make their circuit around it. Neddy commented, indicating Martha and me, with a wide grin, "A polar bear mother with her cub."

Martha wore no bra, had armpit hair, despaired of our present government. Neddy liked to shop at Brooks Brothers, was somewhat sexist, and highly patriotic. I was in between. We loved each other.

When brother and sister embraced and said goodbye, I almost cried. Then Neddy hugged me, and left to catch a bus so he could meet his latest girlfriend. Martha and I wandered back to the bear, then visited the gift shop. We were happy, calm with each other. She bought a T-shirt with piranhas on it for her roommate. We took the bus uptown. It turned out to be the last time the three of us were alone together.

Neddy was donating blood periodically. He said he knew what it was like to be scared there was no good blood around.

He broke up with his newest girlfriend. They never talked to each other about what happened to end their relationship. Neddy was quite depressed over the breakup, beginning to see a pattern. I urged him to talk to the therapist who had helped him before his

"We laughed and laughed."

operation, to try to get a handle on why these relationships didn't last. I said I'd pay for some sessions. Instead, he got a night job at a hotel about a mile from his house.

Everything went along smoothly for a while. Then he lost his job at the bank. When he was fired, it was made clear that his "attitude" was involved. He had told me that sometimes he had trouble with his temper, becoming particularly annoyed about things he considered "stupid." His boss suggested that he see a therapist. Now I wonder if these exaggerated moods were aftereffects from his operation. In any case, I paid for him to go to his old therapist once a week for about six months.

Neddy was already working part time at the hotel as a night clerk, on a shift called Night Audit. After he was fired, he went openly to his employers at the hotel and told them what had happened. He offered to work there full time. He planned to interview for a job in banking, he said, but he guaranteed that he would work at the hotel for six months if they took him on. That's when he started working five days a week at the hotel as a desk clerk, plus all night a couple of nights a week on Night Audit.

Soon after, Neddy met Elizabeth. She was waitressing at the restaurant attached to the hotel while she finished school. She was a year older than he was, twenty-seven. When I met Elizabeth, I liked her. She was very intellectual and focused, and she clearly adored Neddy.

After four months of working at the hotel, Neddy got a job in the loan department at another bank. He kept his job working all night two nights a week at the hotel as well as forty hours a week at the bank. "I'll do it until I get tired of it," he said. I admired his lack of self-pity about himself and about his large doctor's bills. He had health insurance but had to pay the 20 percent that insurance didn't cover. He uncomplainingly took the responsibility, but his expenses were heavier than most new employees, and besides, his rent for his apartment in the converted carriage house was quite high. I discovered later that he had begun to borrow money from his own investment account.

In the fall of 1989, Neddy and I walked through Central Park again. At the zoo, he posed for the last pictures I took of him. He stood by a stone eagle and joked about them both being bald.

On that walk through the park Neddy asked if Martha was gay.

"He posed for the last pictures . . ."

I said she had recently confided that she was. "I thought so," he said. "Maybe someday she'll tell me."

"She will," I answered. We talked about it for a while. A few years earlier, one of his good friends had announced to him that he was gay, and Neddy was extremely shocked. He immediately dumped the friend, but later they renewed their friendship. He was very accepting of Martha.

A few weeks later, Neddy called me on the phone. "I don't know what's going to happen in the future," he said, archly, proudly, happily. I knew he was thinking about marriage.

"Really?" I asked.

"We'll see. Let's not count our chickens before they're hatched. One day at a time!" he cautioned me.

He deserved to be happy, after all he'd been through. I thought it would be wonderful if Neddy got married, had a baby. His relationship with Elizabeth was more solid and committed than any other adult relationship he had ever had. He seemed really joyful. He said his and Elizabeth's personalities and experiences matched up very well.

From a postcard dated January 2, 1990: "HAPPY NEW YEAR! Lots of love, Neddy & Elizabeth. P.S. The run and return trip went fine."

Neddy and Elizabeth planned to train for the New York City Marathon, which was coming up in the fall. To kick off their training, they had run in a four-mile race held at midnight in Central Park on New Year's Eve. I picked up their official race numbers for them at the Road Runner's Club. Neddy had worked all night the night before. It was pouring rain during the race.

Was that when he developed the cough? Certainly he was working hard—all day at the bank, and all Friday and Saturday nights at the hotel.

Soon after that, I saw Neddy to celebrate his twenty-seventh birthday. I was going to take him to Catch a Rising Star, a comedy club, but he was too tired to go and instead went to Ned's apartment to sleep so he would be rested for a seminar he was taking the next day.

At the end of January I wrote in my diary: "We spent yesterday afternoon with Neddy and Elizabeth, going to a children's museum and then eating with them. I was so happy Bill could make it. I knew Neddy wanted us to come as a couple and he and Elizabeth were a couple, and we were all grownups—it was nice. Anyway Bill's sense of humor really enlivened the whole thing. He was putting his head in mirror-lined boxes—in which you could see yourself to infinity—and pulling ropes that released smells, etc. We all ended up in a small hemisphere in the museum that they call a Brainitarium. A little boy had thrown up on the seat so we had to file out while they cleaned up and then come back in to watch a videotape. Neddy had been up all night at the hotel, then had done inventory in a store for a friend, and finally drove in to the city for this outing. I must say, he looked quite well—sometimes exhausted—and was very good-humored and nice with Elizabeth. I don't know how he does it!"

I had been meaning to talk to Neddy about his continuing anger at me for his physical problems, which had emerged at the Christmas pageant, but I knew there was no opportunity because he was so incredibly busy and never got into New York, at least alone.

One day in March I walked out of a local store, and to my

uttermost surprise, there was Neddy running by on the sidewalk! One moment, one second later, and I'd have missed him.

The first cold breath of fear struck then, as his collar was too big for his neck. He'd lost weight, quite a lot of it.

He was in town to replace a contact lens. He walked me up to the church, which was where I was going. We went together into the big sanctuary and sat in a pew.

I took a deep breath and looked up at the cross hanging over the altar for courage.

"I know you're still angry at me," I said. "You were so rude at the pageant at Christmas."

"I *am* still angry at you. I can't get over the feeling that you caused my heart problem, you caused my dyslexia, you caused all the difficult things in my life."

I thought this over.

"Elizabeth's on your side," he added. "She says you love me so much, and you're not responsible because of your alcoholism, but I'm still angry. I've worked through a lot of stuff about my step-mother, I never had anything to work through about Bill, but I just can't shake being angry at you."

"It's important not to deny this, to talk it out, and I want to take responsibility," I said, "but I won't be bludgeoned by you about this. I'm certainly happy Elizabeth is helping you. A therapist could help, too."

"Yeah. My old therapist asked me to do some things to resolve my anger at you, but I found them just too hard and too embarrassing to do. You know, maybe I'm not ready to give up the anger. Because I know I'm not ready to go to any lengths to do it."

He added, endearingly, "I'm not sure I'd *want* to change some of the things that are wrong with me that I blame you for, because they've turned into advantages."

"You know what, Neddy? Your anger isn't hurting *me.* I can hurt myself plenty with my guilt, but your anger hurts *you,* and it holds you back. It also keeps us connected. I don't think you want to be connected to me that way. By the way, I think it's great you're not drinking or drugging and postponing these feelings like I did. You can ask Martha for help. She's worked through a lot of this stuff."

He said he saw no help for it.

"Ultimately," I said, "a power greater than yourself, God, can heal it."

We talked about fetal alcohol syndrome. I said if I could change the fact that I drank when I was pregnant, I would. "I never would want to hurt you. Never. Never," I said. "I love you."

Later, Neddy's thinness haunted me. Something was definitely wrong. I stepped up my contact with him.

A few weeks after our conversation in the church, Neddy and Elizabeth came into the city to get a duvet cover for their comforter. They visited me. I wrote in my diary: "Neddy has lost more weight, so that the bones in his face show. He's been up all night, looks terrible. He's had flu now for two and a half months, gets chills. Now he *can't* eat, or gets a headache when he eats. Elizabeth says recently he worked four or five nights all night at the hotel, as well as his day job. He's *killing* himself. He probably doesn't want to *feel*. This intimate relationship with Elizabeth is probably terrifying him." Neddy's illness, I feared, might really be a case of ACOAism. Adult children of alcoholics often have trouble with many aspects of life.

That night Neddy and Elizabeth went out to dinner with Ned. When they got back, I asked if Ned had said anything about Neddy's health. They answered no.

The next day, I telephoned Dr. K and told him I was worried. He called Neddy and they set up an appointment for the next week. Dr G also scheduled an appointment. Neddy said he would quit his night job if the doctors told him to. He seemed too tied in to making the extra money it provided to make the decision himself. I taped two programs on sleep patterns and what happens when you work all night for long periods of time, and sent them to him.

He called when he had seen both doctors. "They say I'm as healthy as a horse!" he crowed. "I don't have to quit the hotel job." Did I detect a note of puzzlement in his voice?

I remember my own uttermost surprise, and the way I stifled my reaction of disbelief. Obviously, the doctors knew better than I did what was going on.

"Dr. G gave me permission to train for the marathon."

"Huh? That's crazy! Why does he think you can do that? You're sick!"

A coldness came into his voice. "I guess I'm not."

I told myself, *"Neddy's twenty-seven years old now. He's in charge of his life. He's not a little boy. It's up to him to take care of himself. He certainly doesn't want me meddling, that's clear from our experience in the hospital."*

A feeling of unreality began to set in.

A week or so later I ran into Dr. K on the street and told him Neddy was training for the marathon. Dr. K said that that much running was dangerous because the pig valve would wear out faster. He said he would call Dr. G. The next day I phoned his office to remind him to call.

I didn't know then that Neddy had misinterpreted Dr. G's advice. Neddy told me on the phone later that he tried to run and had only traveled twenty yards before exhaustedly turning back.

A few weeks after that, on April 21, I traveled to New Jersey.

Neddy met me at the train station. He looked exhausted and thin. He had worked a regular work week at the bank and then all night the night before at the hotel. I offered to go right back to the city so that he could sleep. He insisted I stay.

While I was there, Neddy received a letter from Dr. K saying he was anemic and to please call for an appointment. Neddy joked that he had AIDS. It was no joke. He looked terrible. I thought it was because he was compulsive about work and skipped meals. I felt angry at Neddy and Elizabeth for acting like everything was normal.

Neddy and I did errands together and had lunch in a sandwich shop. He had a roast beef blimpie, I had minestrone and bread. Then we drove to the mall.

On the way, we had the conversation that rang in my ears for years after he died; I reviewed it again and again. How did it start? What led up to it? I can't remember.

He said, "I want to be cremated. I want to be reduced to my carbon. I want the ashes to be buried, not scattered. I want them buried in the graveyard at Brookfield. Near Grandpop. Near where Daddy'll be buried. I'm not afraid of dying . . . it seems like peace. Don't you ever get tired of struggling?"

I was shocked, but I glanced over at him where he sat in the driver's seat. A miniature black and white soccer ball hanging from the rearview mirror was swaying between us. He was alive, and pink, and breathing, driving the car. The long moment felt deeply intimate and peaceful. I answered, "Don't get too fond of that idea. But I understand."

Later I wondered why I didn't scream and cry and beg him not to talk that way.

It was the last time I saw him.

Back in New York, I called Dr. K. His voice was very serious on the phone. He said he was extremely worried about Neddy. There must be tests. The problem could be a bleeding ulcer.

"Neddy's joking it's AIDS."

"No, it couldn't be that." But then Jim started talking about heterosexual intercourse—so it was clear that he was going to test Neddy for AIDS.

When I hung up the phone, I felt totally crazy. I immediately assumed Neddy had a life-threatening illness.

While I waited, sick with fear and unwilling to admit to Neddy that I had talked to his doctor behind his back, to hear about the tests, which were scheduled for the next week, there were a lot of other things going on.

Four years of intense work in therapy with Kristina was ending because of her retirement to be with her young children full time, and I was suffused with sadness and anxiety. Bill and I were in couples therapy with Kathy, working on extremely painful issues like sex and independence. Looking back, I can see how miserable we were, and that we had begun to hurt each other quite badly. Things had not been right for a couple of years. Our differences and our insecurities were tearing us apart. To top it off, Bill was planning to retire from his teaching career, get the studio, and start his new career as an artist. It was the paramount thing in his life. We were working on keeping the relationship together as this drastic change in our dynamics happened.

There had been a lot of tumult in my life since Bill and I had met six and a half years before. During that time, I had left the company where I'd worked for twelve years, written forty-five published children's books, illustrated ten of them, gone into intensive and painful psychotherapy, commenced menopause, developed a serious alcohol-related hip condition, and coped with Neddy's open-heart surgery.

On April 27, I wrote in my diary: "My appointment with Kristina was taken up with Neddy stuff. She says I'm caught in a web of codependency—I must stop talking to Dr. K behind Neddy's back, *must* tell Neddy that I will not be responsible for worrying about him—or he won't know I am breaking the circle. She says to tell him he's killing himself and he must take the responsibility to get help.

"Kristina said I should say, 'I refuse to take on this worry anymore. It would break my heart if you died, but I can't do anything about your health. You have to do it. I'm resigning the role of informing and warning you. I'm not saying goodbye, I'm just saying you're caught in a web of denial.' I didn't say it, because he didn't call, at least until last night at 11:00 P.M., and then to say the blood test came out 'in the safety range.' He isn't anemic. His chest X-ray is good. He doesn't have an ulcer. He's quit his hotel job, or at least will in two weeks—he'll work there two nights a week until 11:00 P.M. until then.

"Best of all, he's hungry and eating! Dr. K is monitoring his weight. Thank God.

"I must never call Dr. K behind his back again. It was just too horrible to worry that much and to have information that Neddy doesn't have. Also Neddy must have the dignity of being an adult."

Were the bacteria already in his system? Later I heard that they can compartmentalize themselves in the heart so that the only way of finding them is by catheterization.

We didn't usually celebrate Mother's Day in my family because my mother always said it was a manufactured holiday invented by the florist industry. In May 1990, however, Neddy sent me a card. I treasure it as a symbol of the healing between us, although now I wonder how I ever doubted the love between us.

On the front of the card was a quote from Abraham Lincoln: ALL THAT I AM OR HOPE TO BE I OWE TO MY MOTHER.

Inside, Neddy's handwriting scrawled, "Hi! I'm feeling a little bit better each day, and by the time Mother's Day rolls around on Sunday I will be done with Night Audit forever! Thanks! Love, Neddy."

In response, I drew and colored a picture of my children's book character, Danny the Alligator, and sent it off. Danny, representing Neddy, was dressed in an orange coat with gold buttons. He had exhaustion lines under his eyes but he danced a jig and said, "Good-bye, Night Audit! Never again." Night Audit, a strange blue horse with antlers on which were hanging different-colored clock faces with the hands pointing to different hours of the night, headed toward the sunrise calling, "Good-bye." Danny's bed waited for him in the background.

"I drew and colored a picture."

I enclosed a letter informing Neddy that being an adult child of an alcoholic, which I was also, could lead to acting out in destructive ways like workaholism even if he had no problem with drinking. There was no way that he could escape his genetic heritage; I named fifteen people on both sides of his family in several generations who have suffered from alcoholism. I warned about denial, and pointed out that Elizabeth had her own denial about his being sick, because she had lost her father and brother to illness. I cautioned him not to push himself over the edge by trying to prove himself to his father, and finally, suggested he go to a therapist who was knowledgeable about alcoholism and family patterns. I told him I loved him and was proud of him, and sent him some money to help with the doctors' bills.

He still didn't gain weight. On May 15, I sent off cans of protein powder that I bought at the health food store. He mixed the powder with bananas and eggs in a blender and ate the mixture. I also sent the book *Sugar Blues* because he was consuming too many candy bars. He read the book and later we discussed it on the phone.

Near the end of May, Neddy asked me to call my cousin, who lived near him in New Jersey, to ask her for the name of a local physician. While I thought he should call her himself, somehow I ended up doing it. My cousin asked her husband, a retired doctor, for a name. She called me back with one, but made it clear she thought Neddy should go to his own doctors in New York, who knew his case.

I passed along the name of the local doctor to Neddy. We discussed the merits of remaining with his own doctors versus setting up with a new one. I urged him to have both a local doctor and his New York doctors. It would be so much easier if he didn't have to travel to the city all the time.

A week later, Neddy called the local doctor to try to get an appointment. There were none open for several weeks, so he dropped that idea.

On the first weekend that Neddy didn't have to work at the hotel, he and Elizabeth drove up to Boston to see her friends. I was worried about his driving all that way, because he was still sick. Now I can see, he wanted to be normal. He wanted to do normal things.

On May 31, I flew to Las Vegas for a convention and received an award. Then I spent a few days with Martha on Point Reyes in California. I was away six days. The weekend after I got back, Neddy and Elizabeth were staying on Long Island near my cottage.

"Are you going to be there? We could come over," Neddy asked.

I didn't go to Long Island. I stayed in New York, to be with Bill, which was less than satisfactory. We fought.

This is what I torture myself with: if I had seen Neddy that weekend, would he still be alive?

Neddy had scheduled another appointment with Dr. K, who wanted to do another blood test and a GI series because he was convinced that the problem had something to do with the lower tract. On June 11, Neddy left work to go to the appointment, and missed the train. He took the next one, but disembarked in Newark when he realized he was too late to see Jim, who had to leave his office at 2:00 P.M. Neddy made another appointment for Monday, June 18, went home, and slept exhaustedly.

From my diary a few days later: "I talked to Neddy today. He was dreadfully depressed. He isn't gaining weight. His knees hurt when he climbs stairs. He weighs 130. He usually weighs 145. He's very tired. He can't exercise, he's too weak. He has a deep, hacking cough. But Dr. K did a chest X-ray, and there's nothing there obstructing his lungs. I left a message on his answering machine that maybe he has Lyme disease, or Epstein-Barr. E-B has symptoms of fatigue, depression."

I worried all weekend, and spoke to a lot of people, including both my psychotherapists. On the evening of June 18, I called Neddy from a movie theater on Long Island to hear about his appointment with Dr. K.

Neddy announced that he hadn't gone to see Jim at all because his supervisor called him back to do a project just as he was leaving the bank. He didn't want to admit to his boss that he was taking time off again for yet another doctor's appointment, so he meekly went back to do the work and called Jim to cancel the appointment.

"What!" I exclaimed. "Can't Jim see you tomorrow?"

"No, he's going on vacation for the rest of the week. He can't see me until next Monday."

Well, I guess Jim isn't too worried if he's going away. If he were worried, he'd put you in the hospital. He's too good a doctor.

I was furious. "Can't you see his colleague? I can't believe that you're just too people-pleasing to take care of yourself. You should've told your boss that you just HAD to leave!"

"Why are you so angry?" Neddy inquired.

"This just can't go on any longer. I am really frightened."

"I'm not going to die," Neddy soothed me. "I apologize for making it sound so serious. It's not an emergency."

"It isn't? It sure sounds like one."

"Why don't you just leave the worrying to me?" he asked.

"Fine, fine."

"I'll get through the weekend somehow," he added.

"There you go again! Pushing my buttons!"

"Sorry. I won't run or bicycle or do anything. I'll just take care of myself."

"Good. And eat ice cream."

"I just finished a pint."

"Good."

A youth behind me in the movie theater kept tapping me on the shoulder and asking me to get off the phone so he could use it. Couldn't he see I was upset? I turned on him, enraged. "Stop it!" I exclaimed, fiercely. "Just stop it! Can't you see that this is important?"

"Lady, don't be mad," the youth pleaded. "Come on, get off the phone."

"Don't be a fucking asshole!" I yelled into the receiver. "Don't be so fucking stupid! You've got to take care of yourself!"

"I will. I will. Don't worry," Neddy answered.

"Please, please, PLEASE go to the emergency room. It's only half a mile from your house. Do you want me to get the name of a local doctor? I can call Muffie and ask her to call her doctor. Stop it!" I snarled, savagely, to the youth, who was plucking at my sleeve.

"No, I'll be all right. Why don't you call me later if you're so upset?"

"It'll be too late. I'm going over to a friend's house."

"O.K. Don't worry. I'll talk to you soon."

"O.K. I love you."

"I love you, too. Goodbye."

"Goodbye."

That was the last time I talked to him. Ever. Because two days later, I traveled into the city for couples' therapy. When Bill and I got home from the appointment, the message from Dr. Leonard was on my answering machine. It was Wednesday, June 20, 1990, the day Neddy died.

CHAPTER SIXTEEN

Elizabeth wrote me later:

> . . . as is always the case, two people describing the same person or event will recount it differently. . . . certainly my story of Ned and the events leading to his death is different. I *never* thought he looked *that* sick. Reading your account I thought, "Gee, I must have been pretty *stupid* and so must my Mom and his co-workers, the people at the hotel, etc." I've seen people with AIDS who look pretty phthisic and very sick and Ned didn't. We had dinner with his father only a week and a half before and he didn't say or notice anything. To me Ned only looked thin. But as I said, you did seem worried where no one else did. But if Ned looked like some people I've seen with AIDS he probably would have been sent home from work. I *do* resent the comparison but if it's what you were thinking then it is your story and your account. I think of him as healthy one day and dead the next, not on the verge of death for months. Death (or the possibility) never entered my mind.

In late spring of 1991, with the first anniversary of Neddy's death looming closer, I finished my painting of the two boats. It turned out to be full of the most wonderful, vibrant, glowing colors: watermelon, saffron, azure, malachite. I had never done such a big picture before. I hung it at the end of the living room between the windows, and the light pouring in on either side of it made it glow at certain times of day. Sometimes the two elemental shapes of the boats, side by side but not touching, reminded me of Neddy and me, adjacent, silent, neighborly.

"I finished my painting of the two boats."

I had the first dream that I could remember since Neddy had died. In the dream I had children that I'd never met or known about before, French-speaking children, and I stood hugging the twelve-year-old girl for hours, soundlessly, as other people passed through the room.

Later, when I'd left them, I realized I didn't know their names, so I went back to find out. Now the children were adults and lived in New York. I asked them how to spell their names, as a ruse to cover up that I couldn't remember, to save face.

When I woke up I wondered if they were half brother and half sister to Neddy and Martha, and if so, why didn't I remember that I had given birth to them? Later, a friend said they were manifestations of my own inner child.

Easter was late in 1991. As it approached, I pondered the scene at the sepulcher. What could it have been like for Mary to see Christ's dead body, then to find that he was gone—the napkin, the cloth—and then to behold him standing there?

I took the three-foot plastic "lollipop" that I had obtained from a mail-order house that supplied "encounter bats" and "aggression products" and savagely beat the bed, PRETENDING IT WAS ME! (I knew this was self-hatred, but I let myself indulge.) WHAP! POW! TAKE THAT! YOU SHIT, I sobbed, my teeth bared. YOU COULD HAVE SAVED HIM! YOU COULD! ONE MORE PHONE CALL TO DR. K, THAT'S WHAT IT WOULD HAVE TAKEN, AND HE WOULD HAVE GOTTEN ON NEDDY'S *CASE!!!!*

WHY? WHY? WHY? WHY DIDN'T I DO IT?

Gradually, however, I realized that my rage really was focused on HE'S DEAD, AND I CAN'T CHANGE IT. HE'S FUCKING GONE. HE'LL NEVER COME BACK. I'LL NEVER SEE HIM AGAIN.

WHY? WHY? OH GOD, WHY?

I hit the bed some more—WHY DIDN'T HE SAVE HIM-SELF? WHY? IT'S MY FAULT. I MADE HIM DYSFUNC-TIONAL. I DID IT! I DID IT!

Was this pride in reverse? I didn't care.

Finally, I prayed.

"Dear God,

"Help me to lay my guilt and anger at your altar—to give it to you and leave it with you, just for now. Help me to love myself and accept everything I've done, because I always tried my best. Always, even when I was drunk."

God grant me the serenity
To accept the things I cannot change
Courage to change the things I can
And the wisdom to know the difference.

I could not believe, as did Rabbi Kushner, the author of *When Bad Things Happen to Good People,* that death, torture, and all other "bad things" happen outside of God's control. My God was all-powerful, or else he wasn't worth believing in. I had to believe that there is a plan behind everything, that God knows and does all, with his own scheme veiled from us, his dear creatures. I had to believe that, ultimately, God shows us his mercy.

My anger continued after the Easter season passed. I was furious at what many books stated flatly: that love is a bridge to the dead. I could not feel any bridge to Neddy. There was just a blank. The idea seemed like a pitiful human projection.

After the drowning death of his son, Rev. William Sloane Coffin Jr. said many of his fellow ministers offered "comforting words of Scripture" to suggest he find God's will or some blessing in the midst of tragedy. "But the reality of grief is the absence of God," he said, and we must guard against words offered "for self-protection, to pretty up a situation whose bleakness (we) simply (cannot) face . . ."

My therapist Kathy said the anger at religion was the same anger that I had previously aimed at the doctors, at Neddy. That helped to dispel it.

Faith quoted Matthew: "Seek and ye shall find. Ask and ye shall receive. Knock and it shall be opened unto you."

I talked to a minister about my anger at Christ for rising again, when Neddy couldn't. The minister said that Easter was a natural time for grieving persons to be angry—it wasn't unusual at all.

Well, I said, there was something barbaric, primitive, and disgusting about eating the body and blood of Christ, even symbolically. The idea of it made me ill.

He didn't get defensive, but simply replied that the early Christians were often described as cannibals by early detractors in the second century A.D. He added that another way of looking at the sacraments is as fruits of the earth, or renewable resources.

I said I was apoplectic about "Love is Eternal"—that there was no proof, no proof at all, that it is.

When I told him about Neddy wanting to be reduced to his carbon, and how there was a deep peace that passed understanding as we drove in the car, "Isn't *that* 'love is eternal'?" the minister burst out.

We talked about miracles—like the coincidence of my meeting Neddy on the sidewalk outside the photo store—which the minister seemed to define as a miracle—and how a late train might be a miracle to one person and a disaster to someone else. A touchy business, these coincidences.

Later, he said a tender, fervent prayer for "Thy servant, Edith," petitioning for aid in my struggle, for peace, and acceptance. I cried.

I read about the fact that many bereaved parents, after experiencing initial rage at their God, eventually came to the simple acceptance of, "It was God's will. It was part of His plan."

Was I going to be the first parent in the world, the only parent in history, who couldn't find a remedy?

My sister Nancy assured me on the phone, "Neddy will always be with you. Always. But it's not like you planned."

My brother Ken commented, "You're going through the worst thing a parent can endure."

Phil and I talked every week. He didn't say much directly about my grief, but he heeded with compassion as I described each stage I went through, and sometimes listened to me crying on the phone.

Elizabeth and I ate dinner and went to the movies. I felt angry at her before I saw her, and melted when I caught sight of her beguiling face. She remarked that we were very different. (Another time we had talked about being alike.) She didn't want to have children, for instance, and she was not an especially nurturing person. Sure, if Neddy had turned out to be really ill, she said, she would have quit her job and taken care of him. But basically, she simply didn't *want* to ask him if he had eaten lunch, and how he was feeling.

After his operation, Elizabeth said, life was infinitely precious to Neddy. He was fully present in each moment. Just pouring orange juice was a joy. "I'm *so* grateful, every day, that *I* was the one to be with him," she added.

I asked her if they ever talked about getting married.

"Often."

And children?

"I didn't want to have them, but for a mad week after he died, I hoped I was pregnant."

Oh, God. That stopped me cold. I tried to imagine it. His baby. It would be born by now.

She told him even though she didn't want children that if he were dying (ever), she would want his baby.

They hoped to spend the rest of their lives together.

"I'll never get married, now," Elizabeth said.

"Never say never."

A theologian had told her that marriage is the only sacrament that can be celebrated without benefit of a priest. Just as there are "baptisms-by-desire" throughout the ages, when the intention is there, he said, so there are marriages-by-desire when the intention is there, and she ought to consider that she had experienced one.

"I don't want to idealize him," she said. "I've recently come to know that he was way off base about money. Having that second job was wrong. I was too timid about telling him I wanted more of him for myself. I thought it was wrong to complain."

"We are so lucky to have her," I said later to Martha about Elizabeth on the phone. "She is a wonderful, wonderful person."

"Neddy was lucky to have her," Martha said.

Martha's thirtieth birthday was coming up. She still felt like she was floundering in an enormous ocean of grief, with no land in sight, and unable to imagine that land would be secure if she ever did find it. She said she'd been dreaming about Neddy again. I decided to give her "land" for her birthday, but how? A necklace with a pendant of an island on it? Earrings? Eventually I painted a headland (for the land should not stand alone), with a beach, trees, a little house, a small human figure on the beach, and a sailboat sailing in the bay. High above, violet light peeked through a break in the clouds. I framed, packaged, and mailed the painting, with a note reading, "This present is Land. Really it's to perch on. It is solid ground."

I drove up to Connecticut on a foggy, rainy day to visit Neddy's grave. Carrying some gladiolas and remembering my mother-in-law cutting "glads" in her nearby garden, I climbed the hill, coming upon the sandy grave with a faded soggy bouquet lying on it, hearing the earthmoving machines roaring in the sandpit. I stayed only a short while.

Elizabeth graduated from college, which she had attended at night while working full time in the daytime. She wrote me a letter:

. . . I love the Tennyson poem that [the graduation speaker] quoted. "Not to Yield" reminded me of Ned and his determination which I always admired and which I think I now possess in part. It is really quite an inheritance because with it I know I can be successful. When the president asked us to turn around and thank the people who had made the momentous occasion possible I thought I couldn't thank the one person who made it possible for me because he was not there. It was sad . . . but I realized that you were there and it was your love and concern that played such a part in Ned's life and that made him the wonderful person he was, with so much to give to me. So I thanked you and in that moment I was *really* glad you were there (even though I couldn't see you). In fact afterwards when I couldn't find you outside I wondered if I had just imagined you were there. I was glad to finally see you . . .

A few weeks later, she called to tell me she had gotten into divinity school. Soon after, Martha announced she had been accepted into a graduate writing program at a university in New York. She was one of thirty chosen out of 600 applicants. "You know," she commented, "Neddy wouldn't be so pleased about my getting into grad school—he was always jealous of how easily things came to me, academically at least." She decided to use his life insurance money, which he had bequeathed to her, to go to school.

In early June I moved out to the cottage on Long Island for the summer. I tacked a poster of Derain's *The Red Sails* to the wall in my bedroom. The first morning I slept there, a pheasant's squawks woke me at 5:45 A.M., and slatted early light coming through the blind was falling across the poster.

When I stepped outside the cottage door, the sky was full of Turneresque clouds—puffy, with highlights of mauve, blue, green. I walked around outside the cottage with my toast and peanut butter, looking at everything, checking everything out. Two huge swans passed overhead, necks outstretched, wings beating, "Whop! Whop!" Rabbits nibbled the lawn. I clumped along in my nightgown, bed socks, and old running shoes which quickly grew wet with the dew.

Later I rode my bike around my square. The bridge was closed for repairs and the town and the township were squabbling over who owned it and who should fix it. I threaded my way past the barriers meant to keep people off, and stopped in the middle of the span. A lone swan stood up in the water and flapped its wings. At the general store, I stopped for the newspaper, forty cents already counted out in my shorts pocket. I bought stamps at the post office. "Welcome back," the postmaster greeted me, with a big grin.

Martha finally received the birthday package containing my painting of "Land" in its gilt frame. Crying, she left a message on my answering machine about how much it meant. "The best part is that it means *you* will be land."

I had found out months before that the author and spiritual teacher Stephen Levine would be leading a workshop on "Healing Into Life and Death" in New York a few days before the first anniversary of Neddy's death, and had sent away for a ticket.

The workshop was held in a seedy ballroom on the seventh floor of the old New Yorker Hotel on Thirty-fourth Street and Eighth Avenue. Stephen, a gentle, unpretentious man, sat on the stage and spoke into a mike. There were 900 people in the ballroom, many of them from health professions, and AIDS patients, people with other illnesses, and those who were bereaved.

I wrote down some of the things Stephen said on the first day:

"Grief is the rope-burn in our hands from trying to keep someone from going."

"Grief is holding, hardness, lack of forgiveness."

"The sharing of grief is the path of joy."

"Guilt is anger turned inward."

"It is not 'your' guilt; it's 'the' guilt—a universal condition."

"To the degree that we back away from life now, we will when we die."

"The secret of life is 'pay attention.' "

The healing referred to in the title of the workshop was not necessarily healing of the body, but healing of the mind, which involves opening the heart. During the meditation on forgiveness that he led in the afternoon, Stephen told us to let back into our hearts someone whom we had closed out. Up until then I hadn't known that I'd closed Neddy out, that all my anger at him for dying and my guilt that I hadn't saved him left no room for him in my heart. I welcomed him back, and sobbed. Later in the meditation Stephen asked us to imagine someone who had closed us out of their heart, and I realized I had shut myself out of my own heart, by blaming myself. In a few moments, I drifted off to sleep.

On the second day I arrived early and put my mat on the floor in the area in front of the seats, about twenty feet away from the stage. The floor was soon crowded with bath towels, rugs, meditation stools, deck chairs, and people.

Some things Stephen said on the second day:

"Let him go. Let him die. Forgive him."

"Help him to finish his journey—send him on. Say goodbye, which means, 'God be with you.' Ask for his forgiveness. Send him forgiveness."

"The hardest work we will ever do is to let go of our suffering."

"Guilt says, 'I am an asshole, I deserve to suffer . . .' "

"The mind is involuntarily merciless with itself."

We did a meditation on death. Before we started, Stephen described the process of dying, as reported by people who had been resuscitated.

The first stage is that physical pain goes away. Feeling leaves the body.

Next, the body becomes immobile, although awareness remains.

Then, the circulation closes down and there is an expansiveness, a flowing outward.

Many people who return from this stage report a light.

"What happens next I don't know," said Stephen.

He compared dying to an ice cube, which starts out with very defined borders. Then, as it melts, its boundaries become blurred. It flows out into a puddle, then is absorbed into the air.

When I thought about dying, I realized that it is just as natural as any other human function. And it certainly isn't unique; fifty million humans do it every year. Each stage is programmed. Everything is already worked out.

At the end of the workshop, I had the good fortune to talk to Stephen as he sat on the edge of the ballroom stage.

"My son died a year ago," I started off.

"Oh, of what?" he asked, gently.

My face twisted. "A . . . a bacteria in his heart."

"Ohhhh. I'm sorry."

"Endocarditis?" inquired a man standing next to me in the crowd around the stage.

"No. It was a strep."

"You must miss him terribly," Stephen said, compassionately, looking me full in the face, focusing all of his attention on me.

"I do. And I keep going over and over and over it. Because he was sick for four months. And the doctors didn't catch it. He worked until the day he died. And he kept getting sicker and sicker . . ."

"Did you know something was wrong?"

"Yes."

"You weren't ready for that."

"No," I answered, but then mused, "But maybe *he* was. Because . . . because the last time I saw him, which was about a month before he died, we were driving in the car, and he said, I mean, he wasn't supposed to be sick but we both knew he was, and he said, 'I want to be cremated. I want to be reduced to my carbon. I want the ashes to be buried, not scattered.' He said, 'I want them to be buried in, in a certain graveyard. I'm not afraid of dying. It seems like peace. Don't you ever get tired of struggling?' "

Stephen broke out into a smile. "Pretty good," he said. "Pret-ty good."

I grinned proudly. "I know."

"How did you feel when he said that?"

"I, uh, I felt fine. It was okay, just for then, and I told him so. Of course, later . . ."

"See? It's the mind again. See how the mind is merciless? We do the right thing, we know what to do, you knew what to do, how to react. Then the mind comes in and tells us we're wrong."

"Yes. But . . ."

"Just miss him, that's all, just miss him."

"I wish I could 'just' miss him, but all this guilt and anger gets in the way."

Stephen leaned toward me, gazing even more deeply into my eyes. "He may have been born for that moment," he said. "How could he stick around after that? He didn't have to stay any more."

I reeled, stunned with the enormity of what he was saying. He continued. "Ninety-five percent of the people in this room long for such a moment of acceptance with a parent like you. Were you here yesterday? Did you see how few people in the audience raised their hand when I asked how many people believe they were born into their own family? Only about 10 percent. Well, your son chose the right mother. He chose to be born to the right mom. You chose each other. And, after that perfect moment, he didn't need to stay any longer. How could he stay?"

"I can't believe what you're saying to me," I said, on the verge of tears, and deeply moved, and believing him. "It *was* a perfect moment. I've never felt such peace."

"Do you have other children?"

"Yes. One. A daughter."

"How is she?"

"She's been in terrible grief. Now she's decided to use the life insurance money my son left her to move East and go to graduate school here. We are very close, too."

"Have fun with her."

"I will."

I told him that I was an alcoholic, eighteen years sober, and that I drank when I was pregnant, and used that to flagellate myself, too.

"It's hard, with addiction, because of the self-hatred. I was an addict," he stated, and laughed. "Here we are, wounded healers," he added.

We looked deep into each other's eyes for a few long moments. "He chose the right mother," Stephen murmured, then leaned down, reverently kissed the back of my hand, then released it. I turned away to leave the group of people clustered around him.

On the first anniversary of Neddy's death, I woke up on Long Island.

A mourning dove cooed as I left the cottage for my ride and a tiny rabbit ran in circles on the lawn. Its mother ate stolidly, chewing fast. Buttercups bloomed by the roadside. Pheasants skittered away as I passed. The far-stretching fields and the arc of the sky brought a deep peace after the claustrophobia of the city.

Potato plants were "filling in," touching each other across the furrows. At the beach there were huge rollers. Two surfers in wetsuits bobbed out where the waves began to break. A heavy, sweet smell of honeysuckle enveloped me as I left the beach. I bicycled past a field of yellow rye. Barn swallows swooped low, paddling with their wings, darting after mosquitoes. I bought the newspaper, rode on the mottled sidewalk, passed the schoolhouse and the parsonage, turned into my street, coasted down the driveway.

Later, I called Pema. She was still in retreat for another week. When I hung up, the phone rang, and it was my brother Phil, calling to say he was thinking of me.

"You are resilient," he said.

"Something is helping me," I answered. "Thank you for being there—this year—and always."

I settled down on the sofa to talk to Neddy.

Neddy, my dearest, I'm wearing the T-shirt you gave me. Its message reads, INSANITY IS HEREDITARY—YOU GET IT FROM YOUR KIDS.

I could use some of your insanity—foolishness—humor—joy. Last night I said to someone, "I hope I'm not living in a fool's paradise, concerning the lightness I feel, the release, the glee." She answered, "Well, for sure, you are *living in a fool's paradise!" The world.*

Stephen Levine (from *Meetings at the Edge*) ". . . the form which seemed so important but is now denied you may be seen . . . as an illusion which in some ways kept you separate. Separate from the most profound, silent, inner penetration of each other. In an odd way you can go beyond the forms that always kept you separate, of mother and [son], of elder and child, of someone who knew and someone who had something to learn. [Now] the essence of being is shared in love and the grief will burn its way to completion. [He] is gone now into [his] next perfect evolutionary step, just as the unbearable pain you feel propels you toward your next stage of life and being."

Neddy. I'm sitting here—the mourning dove cooing—eating plums, your favorite. I bought this rope bracelet at the store. The paper that came with it describes it this way: "The decorative weave in this sailor's wristlet was used in sailing ship days. Traditionally the wristlets were allowed to shrink on the wearer's wrist to a snug fit." Yes! You wore that rope bracelet we got in Nantucket for years—how many years? Five? We had to cut it off, finally.

"I remember playing catch with you . . ."

I remember playing catch with you in the field between these cottages, about fifteen years ago—a wonderful *game of catch, lasting a* long *time. Grounders, fliers, hard pitches that thumped into our mitts. We tossed and called to each other until the shadows grew long across the grass and it was time to go home.*

I'm holding in my hand a copy of that toast that you gave on Christmas morning. You said, "O.K. So I really blew it sometimes. As a matter of fact if one is going to count the times, you will need more than eight fingers and two thumbs."

Neddy. Listen to me. You never blew it. And if you did, I forgive you.

Now I'm going to say goodbye.
"Goodbye" means "God be with you."
I am not abandoning you. You are not abandoning me. On the contrary.
You and I are together in this, along with everyone and everything else.
Go with my love.
Go into the Light.
You *knew.*
"Reduced to my carbon."
The whale, the man in the plane with the ashes, you running on the sidewalk when I came out of the store, "I'll love you forever."
Now is the perfect moment.
All the "What if's" and the "I should have's" are gone.
I'm frightened.
But that's just the merciless mind.

AFTERWORD

In the several years since that first goodbye, there have been others.

As time has passed, my rage and guilt have lessened, and I can think of Neddy's last days without feeling that I should have saved him. I can look at the tragedy of what happened, and experience the sadness. Sometimes I don't even feel sadness. I may even go for days without thinking of him at all. At other times, I cry, but not as often as I used to. I don't beat the bed anymore. (Much.)

The books talk about unresolved grief and the endless interrogations that parents impose upon themselves. This self-torture can lead to distorted grief, which may linger in one form or another for a lifetime.

Guilt and anger are normal, because the loss of a child is different from any other loss. Often the main component of a parent's grief is guilt or anger.

I've stopped feeling sad on Wednesdays, and no longer mark the twentieth of every month, but I still have Neddy's telephone number in New Jersey programmed into my phone, sometimes I search for a glimpse of him on the street, and occasionally I talk out loud to him when I'm alone. Perhaps I am closer, partly through writing this book, to something that seemed unattainable when I first read about it: remembering Neddy with joy, or at least equanimity.

206

Holidays continue to be difficult. Martha, who moved back to New York to attend graduate school, and I went to the Christmas pageant at the church a couple of times. One year there weren't any sheep in the cast. "Maybe Neddy took them with him," I whispered to Martha, "along with his car." Neddy's beloved red Toyota, which he drove to the hospital and left on the street, was never found. Martha joked that Neddy took it with him, he loved it so much. Other years we traveled at Christmas, partly to avoid the pageant.

Necrosis, probably brought on by my long-ago drinking, had finally destroyed the head of my femur, and I underwent hip replacement surgery. Martha spent nights with me after I got home, helping me to wash, turn over in bed, and cook meals. The operation was a success: now I regularly walk ninety city blocks.

Martha talked of her sadness that our family would die out because she probably won't have children. Sometimes I feel angry at her for being a lesbian and taking away my hopes for grandchildren. But eventually I resolved this by thinking about family trees. In most of them some branches simply end, while others continue to grow. Besides, I know on a deep level that the path Martha is choosing for herself is the right one for her.

Martha and I get together at least once a week when she comes over to give me a massage. The feeling of her hands moving calmly, professionally over my body in a predictable pattern, starting with my back and ending with my face and head, is deeply soothing. Afterwards, we have dinner. We eat the same things almost every time: chicken, baked potato, peas. Food from her childhood, and my own.

Martha is working on her thesis, a book-length collection of stories. One of them is about the everyday violence in the characters' lives and how they have become numb to it. Another is about the death of a sister. It's not surprising that both of us—I've written a children's novel in which a character dies—are dealing with death and mourning in our creative efforts. After all, we know the territory inside out.

Sometimes I go into a panic when I imagine that Martha is in danger. My fear that something will happen to her has increased since Neddy's death. Martha accommodates me, but at a certain point, she tells me to cut it out.

Occasionally, my faith in God seems to vanish. Sometimes I stop meditating and praying, but almost every day I do QiGong exercises, which are physical exercises for my back and hip that I learned from a Chinese master after my operation. I try to practice them in the mindful way that the master taught me: "Wild Geese Roosting," "Three Circles to Heaven," "Holding Up the Sky," "Gazing Back," "Bear Walk," "Harmonizing the Six Realms." Sometimes, grasping nothing between my hands—"Bear Walk"—I thrust them into the sunlight on the cottage wall. The shadow of my hands is the visible sign that I am alive. Time does not hold still but the ecstasy is timeless and I forget myself. *"Relieve me of the burden of self, that I may better do Thy will."* Or, on the beach, watching a wave drain back into the sea, I am that water, those floating bubbles, enraptured, fully there, at one. At other times, I do the QiGong exercises while watching TV, which ruins the meditation aspect.

When I told Stephen Levine at another workshop about the QiGong and the joy he said, "You're teaching your son something through that joy. It's painful that he's dead, but on some level, it feels right, doesn't it?" I read in a book about the small kernel of relief that exists when someone who has been sick dies, when one doesn't have to worry anymore.

C.S. Lewis talks about the shame in feeling better. He says sometimes we hold on to grief out of vanity, to prove the extent of our love. He also says we can experience a confusion: sometimes we think we are preserving a relationship with the dead by holding on to our pain.

I dreamed about Neddy for the first time about two years after his death. We were in a large and dusty museum with high, glassed-in walls (like a conservatory), sprigs of bamboo in large urns, and deserted galleries. We sat together on a stone bench and talked. He was absolutely himself, and happy. The wonderful feeling of being with him was completely familiar.

Elizabeth and Martha visit the graveyard together each year, and we three get together on Neddy's birthday.

A year and a half after Bill left, I was still alternating between missing him and condemning him, so I wrote him a letter in which I took responsibility for my part in the relationship's not working out. Clearly, in retrospect, it was not going right even before

Neddy died, and I was not happy. Perhaps Bill and I would have eventually been able to end our relationship mutually, but Neddy's death interrupted the process. I received a touching letter from Bill in reply to mine saying that he owed me an amend, and that he prayed for me, Neddy, and Martha every night. About a year later I met him on the street and he told me he was married.

I've been out on dates and had a chance or two to become involved since Neddy died, but I've chosen so far to be alone. I realize it might take me a long time to trust enough to get involved with a man—and there aren't too many candidates around. I've come to appreciate my male friends more than ever; talking on the phone, going to the movies, having dinner. My life is very full and I am content most of the time. Sometimes, though, I feel lonely.

One summer, on the spur of the moment, I dined with my ex-husband and his wife at their house. It was a generous gesture on their part. As we ate, I acknowledged God and the healing that had taken place, and Neddy and Martha in my heart.

Pema and I got together in Boston. She had had three deaths since I had left the abbey. "Death is teaching me—trying to unlock the places where I'm still shut."

Therapy with Kathy ended two years after Neddy died when Kathy urged me to terminate. I didn't need her, she said; I had many other resources and used them well. It felt good to decide to end therapy after all the involuntary decisions that had been imposed on me from the outside.

I gave two parties, one on Long Island and one in New York, to thank friends for their loving support. Each party could have been twice as large. It took a lot of courage to celebrate my life without Neddy. I had a good time.

A fund to support dyslexic students or faculty members who help them was established at Pomfret. Neddy's class donated in his memory a wooden bench, which was installed near the goal at the soccer field. A plaque reads, IN MEMORY OF NED DAVIS—A TRUE FRIEND AND CLASSMATE WHO LOVED POMFRET SCHOOL.

One summer I flew to South Dakota, rented a car, and drove north on a road that paralleled the state's western border. The countryside was stark, beautiful, and mostly empty; buttes and plains and dry waddies with putty-colored sheep standing around parched water holes. As I traveled north on the arrow-straight road, amber and emerald-green fields in checkerboard blocks began to predominate. Crops harvested in patterns of lines contrasted with gray wooden houses, battered by wind and often leaning over, abandoned by the roadside. I thought of all the hope and hard work that had gone into building them and their barns and outbuildings, and how life was just too difficult and the winters too bitter in this windswept place to go on.

I was on my way to see the Catholic chaplain who had comforted me in the hospital when Neddy had his operation. At that time the chaplain had been a student whose summer job was working at the hospital. Now he had graduated from school and had a parish of his own in rural North Dakota.

When we finally met, it was almost anticlimactic. The journey, arduous and parched, seemed almost more important than the destination. I had anticipated that this priest would impart wisdom about spirituality, about faith, and, indeed, we had long talks about theology, but it turned out we were equals in our respective quests. I visited his church in a tiny town (pop. 300) which was dominated by a huge grain elevator on a railway spur, and met his parishioners. In the end the visit taught me more about friendship than about some lofty pronouncement from on high, and putting people on pedestals seemed even more futile than before.

In an effort to figure out what I believed about the afterlife, I continued to read about death. One book was about terminal patients, who, as death nears, often see long-dead relatives waiting for them. Also people who have died and have been revived often report seeing dead relatives. However, another book "proved" that near death experiences (the out-of-body experience, the tunnel, the light) are caused by a lack of oxygen to certain areas of the brain and can be stimulated mechanically. Whether such a phenomenon is supernatural or physical, I still cling to the hope that I will see Neddy again.

While I've done a great many things to assuage the grief, I know in a sense it will always be there. I'll always miss my son. I also realize that I've been changed irrevocably by his death and by what happened after it. Letting in the grief helps to dispel it faster, of that I have no doubt. In some ways, I'm still the insecure, anxiety-driven person I was before, and in other ways I see things differently now: I'm lighter and more open to life and to joy than ever before.

After my operation I still had some physical problems that were caused by my posture and by the way I walked. My hips seemed locked, I leaned forward at the waist, my chin protruded, my feet shuffled. I had to learn to walk a new way. That's what I continue to do; learn to walk a new way.

Books That Helped Me

(A Partial List)

The Day Gone By by Richard Adams
The Responsibility Trap by Claudia Bepko
When Good-bye Is Forever by John Bramblett
Final Gifts by Maggie Callanan & Patricia Kelley
Stronger Than Death by Sue Chance, M.D.
The Grief Recovery Handbook by John W. James and Frank Cherry
The Wisdom of No Escape by Pema Chodron
Grief: Climb Toward Understanding by Phyllis Davies
Holy the Firm by Annie Dillard
Tracks by Louise Erdrich
I Dreamed of Africa by Kuki Gallmann
"The Blessing," from *The Portable Graham Greene*
Death Be Not Proud by John Gunther
Sketches from a Life by George Kennan
Beyond Endurance by Ronald J. Knapp
When Bad Things Happen to Good People by Harold S. Kushner
A Gradual Awakening by Stephen Levine
Healing into Life and Death by Stephen Levine
Meetings at the Edge by Stephen Levine
Who Dies by Stephen Levine
A Grief Observed by C.S. Lewis
Hour of Gold, Hour of Lead by Anne Morrow Lindbergh

Anna: A Daughter's Life by William Loizeaux
The Habit of Being by Flannery O'Connor
Closer to the Light by Melvin Morse, M.D., with Paul Perry
The Courage to Grieve by Judy Tatelbaum
How to Go On Living When Someone You Love Dies by Rando Therese
The Animal Wife by Elizabeth Marshall Thomas
Reindeer Moon by Elizabeth Marshall Thomas
The Lives of a Cell by Lewis Thomas
Notes of a Biology Watcher by Lewis Thomas
The First Year of Forever by B.D. Van Vechten
The Holy Bible King James Version
Necessary Losses by Judith Viorst
Lament for a Son by Nicholas Wolterstorff

Grief Groups

The Compassionate Friends
National Headquarters
P.O. Box 3696
Oak Brook, IL 60522-3696
(708-990-0010)

The Compassionate Friends
Manhattan Chapter
Marble Collegiate Church
3 West 29th Street
New York, NY
(212-517-9820)